THE
UNDERGROUND
REPORTERS

—KATHY KACER—

Evans

First published in the UK in 2007 by
Evans Brothers Ltd
2A Portman Mansions
Chiltern St
London W1U 6NR

Published by permission of Second Story Press,
Toronto, Ontario, Canada

British Library Cataloguing in Publication Data

Kacer, Kathy, 1954-
    The underground reporters
    1. Jewish children - Czech Republic - Budejovice - Juvenile
    literature 2. World War, 1939-1945 - Jews - Juvenile
    literature 3. World War, 1939-1945 - Children - Czech
    Republic - Juvenile literature 4. World War, 1939-1945 -
    Czech Republic - Juvenile literature 5. World War,
    1939-1945 - Press coverage - Juvenile literature
    I. Title
    940.5'3161'0922

ISBN-13: 9780237531591
ISBN-10: 0237531593

The photographs used in this book were contributed by the following
people: Kathy Kacer, Jirka Kende, Hana Kende and Frances Nassau.
The photographs of Klepy are from the Jewish Museum in Prague.
The photograph of Adolf Hitler reviewing his troops, as well as the
three maps of Czechoslovakia, are from the United States Holocaust
Memorial Museum.

For John Freund, with gratitude and admiration,
and for my children,
Gabi and Jake

Contents

Prologue

Leaving Home, April 14, 1942

On Tuesday, April 14, 1942, John Freund awoke as he did every morning. He got up, ate breakfast with his family, buttoned his clean white shirt, and put on his jacket. But on this day everything else was different because he was going on a journey. John licked his hand and smoothed down his short, brown, wavy hair, his dark eyes round and uncertain. He took a deep breath and glanced around at the room he had shared with his brother, Karel, for his whole life – almost twelve years. John's football rested in a corner of the room, along with his table tennis paddle. He was leaving these and other prized possessions behind for this journey. There would be no toys where he was going.

At any other time, the thought of a trip would have been exciting. But these were not ordinary times, and John and his family had no choice about leaving. Why are we being forced out of our home? he wondered. We haven't done anything wrong. But these days, his parents just turned away when he asked hard questions. "Hurry up, John," his mother called from the kitchen. She was wrapping up the rolls she had just baked. We can't take very much with us, she thought grimly, but we still have to eat.

John's father entered the kitchen, glancing sadly at his wife. "I'm taking my doctor's bag with me after all," he announced, "even though they haven't let me treat patients here for some time. The medicines and medical equipment may come in handy wherever we end up."

His wife nodded and turned back to the food she was packing. "It's time to leave, John," she called.

John looked down at his bed, piled high with his belongings. Fifty kilograms of luggage was not very much. Should he take books or clothing? If they were going to be away over winter, he would need warm clothes. He tossed one more jumper into his suitcase and closed it, took another deep breath, and picked up his case. Then John and his family walked out of their home for the last time.

In another part of town, Ruda Stadler was also worrying about what to take when he left home. Most of all, he was worried about the newspapers. There were twenty-two editions of the newspaper, and hundreds of hours had gone into making them. He stared down at the collection. I have to do something with these, he thought desperately. I have to find a way to keep them safe.

"What are we going to do with these?" asked Ruda as his older sister, Irena, entered the room.

"We could take them with us," she suggested.

"No," said Ruda, "I don't think that's a good

idea." He didn't know what was going to happen to his family, but he knew things were not going to be good. There was too much uncertainty ahead – too many rumours about terrible conditions and harsh treatment. Besides, the collection of newspapers weighed a lot. He needed the space in his suitcase for clothing and other supplies. "But we can't just leave them here."

These were more than just newspapers. They contained the thoughts and ideas of many young people, who had written about the daily events of their lives and their dreams for the future. Despite the hardships of the previous years, Ruda and his friends had poured their hearts into these papers. They had tried, through their writing, to look at life optimistically. They held hope for a peaceful world to come. All of this was reflected in these twenty-two editions; this collection was their legacy. If Ruda left the papers behind in his home, they might be destroyed. If he took them with him, they might still be lost.

Finally, Ruda and Irena came up with a plan. It was the best solution they could think of, and Ruda hoped and prayed that the newspapers would be safe. Still, saying goodbye to the newspapers was like saying goodbye to his best friend.

All across town, Jewish families walked out of their homes that day, leaving behind their precious belongings – paintings, books, dishes, clothing and furniture. Their destination was Theresienstadt, the concentration camp where they were to be imprisoned. They did not know how long they would be away, or what conditions would be like in Theresienstadt. They tried not to think too much about the future. They were worried enough about what they were leaving behind, without tormenting themselves about what they might find ahead. They had their families, at least. A few young children whimpered but mostly the families moved silently toward the factory in town where they would spend the next few days, waiting for trains that would take them to Theresienstadt. One thousand Jewish people walked across town that day, all of them lost in their own thoughts.

As he moved through the quiet streets, carrying his suitcase, John looked up at the strained faces of his parents. They were trying to pretend that everything would be fine, but he didn't believe them. He didn't like to see them looking so anxious. It made him afraid, and he didn't want to be scared. Maybe the move to Theresienstadt would be an adventure, he thought, trying, as he always did, to be positive. Since the swimming hole had closed and they had stopped writing the newspaper, things had become so lonely in town.

Thoughts of the newspaper and the swimming hole suddenly filled John's mind, and memories came rushing back to him. It's a funny thing about memories, he realised. You can't stop them once they start. They're like water flowing freely from a tap; like the fast-flowing waters of the river by the swimming hole where he and his good friends had spent the happiest times he could remember, playing games, forming close friendships, and creating the newspaper that would become the focus of their energy and imagination. For John, walking away from everything he knew, the memories were suddenly overwhelming. He remembered back to 1939 – not so long ago – when all of this had begun.

THE
UNDERGROUND
REPORTERS

John and his family lived on the second floor of this apartment building.

Chapter 1
Introducing John

About 150 kilometres south of Prague, the capital city of the country that was once called Czechoslovakia, there is a town called Budejovice (pronounced Boo-day-ho-vee-tsay). The Czech king Premsyl Otakar II established the town a long time ago, in 1265. It lies in a valley where the rivers Vltava and Malse (pronounced Mal-sheh) come together and encircle the entire town, like a giant moat around a castle.

In the centre of town is a broad plaza called the Square of King Premsyl Otakar II, paved with cobblestones and surrounded by multicoloured buildings, fruit and vegetable stalls, and vendors selling their wares. In the middle of the square is a tremendous fountain; when it was constructed, back in 1721, it was the town's water supply. A statue of Samson taming a lion dominates the centre of the fountain. In another corner of the square rises the hugely tall Black Tower with its clock and bell that chimes out every hour.

In the 1930s, Budejovice was a small city with many businesses, schools, restaurants and theatres, and the bustling traffic of trams, carts, cars, and pedestrians. At that time, there were about fifty thousand people living there. Of that number, approximately one thousand were Jewish. The people of the Jewish community had all sorts of jobs: they owned small businesses, and they were doctors, teachers, artists and salespeople. Some were wealthy and some were poorer. But even the poor Jewish families lived in pleasant small apartment buildings and had enough money to live comfortably. All of these families lived, worked, and went to school together with their Christian neighbours. Although there was a small population of very religious Jews who followed strict Jewish traditions, most of the Jewish families lived much the same lives as the rest of the town.

John Freund was born in this lovely medieval town on June 6, 1930. By the time he was nine years old, he had grown into a slender boy with a full head of thick, curly brown hair and deep-set dark eyes. More than anything, John loved sports, particularly football, and for his age and size he was fit and muscular. His father, Gustav, was a pediatrician, and his office was just a fifteen-minute walk from the family apartment. John loved to pretend that he was sick just so his father would spend time doctoring him, as he did the many sick children he attended so lovingly. John's mother, Erna, stayed at home to look after the family. She was a cultured woman who knew all about poetry and music. John loved going shopping with her, especially when she headed for the market in town. The best part of the trip came at the end. If John was lucky and well-behaved, he was rewarded with a fresh roll heaped with thinly sliced meat – his favourite treat.

Karel was three years older. He could be a bully, and he was often mean to John, grabbing things from him or hitting him for no apparent reason. One day, when John was just seven years old, Karel locked him in the yard next to their apartment building. "Karel, let me out!" John yelled. He kicked the tall gate and

John aged nine.

shouted, "I'll tell Mother and Father if you don't let me out." On the other side of the gate, Karel laughed. He wasn't afraid of his young brother or his parents. Karel was tough and rebellious, not at all like the milder-mannered John.

But to John this was no longer funny. By now, he was scared. In desperation, he bent down, picked up a heavy rock, and heaved it over the gate. It hit its target, smashing into Karel's head and causing him to bleed quite badly. Karel was taken to the hospital for stitches, and John was in serious trouble.

"This is inexcusable!" his father exploded. "What on earth were you thinking when you threw that rock?"

John tried to protest – after all, Karel had started the whole thing by locking him in the yard in the first place. But his parents would not listen. They even asked their rabbi, Rudolph Ferda, to talk to John about his behaviour.

"What if there had been a mother wheeling a pram past when you threw that rock?" demanded Rabbi Ferda.

The rabbi was a kind and sensitive man, well liked by everyone in town, and his scolding embarrassed John. John stared at him, but found it hard to listen to what the rabbi was saying. Instead, he focused on the rabbi's full mouth of teeth, all painted gold to prevent cavities. Besides, John was secretly pleased with himself for finally standing up to Karel.

For the most part, John was better behaved than Karel, but not always. He could create his own share of trouble. One day, for example, John had a few friends over. The Freund family lived in a four-room apartment on the second floor of a four-story building in an attractive part of town. Their apartment was spacious and beautifully decorated, with dark wooden floors, high arching ceilings, and large bright windows. John shared his bedroom with Karel. When John looked out his bedroom window, he could see the red brick of his school just two blocks away.

That day, John's mother was out shopping and his father was at his office, attending to his patients. "You may have your friends over to visit, but make sure everyone is well-behaved," John's mother had warned as she had left for the market. John had nodded, happy for the opportunity to be left alone. He was young to be in the apartment by himself, but – like most children at that time – he was given a lot of freedom. There were few dangers in Budejovice, and most of his neighbours knew him and would watch out for him if there was trouble.

John's friends arrived and started playing a wild game of tag, and the warning from John's mother was instantly forgotten. The boys made so much noise that someone in the building notified the landlady, a sour old woman named Mrs. Kocher. Up the stairs she waddled, pounding on the Freund apartment door.

"Let me in, now!" she demanded. Inside, the boys froze. No one dared open the door. Finally Mrs. Kocher pushed through the door and the boys scattered, climbing onto furniture and hiding behind chairs. Waving a big, bristly broom, Mrs. Kocher chased John out of the closet and around the dining-room table, whacking him sharply whenever he was within range!

Another stern lecture from John's parents followed this adventure.

Life was lively for John growing up in Budejovice. And he did all the things that young people his age loved to do. He played marbles on the pavement, close to the blacksmith shop. He played football and hockey on the street in front of his apartment building. He was a good football player and could easily outrun the other children. He went ice-skating at the local arena. He sometimes took the tram that wound its way through town, toward the square and beyond it, to the northern part of the city.

"Be careful on the tram," his parents warned him. "Don't get off until it comes to a complete stop." But John was young and daring, and he ignored his parents. He would wait until the tram slowed down, and then leap into the air, hoping to land feet first. That didn't always happen. Often he would tumble onto the pavement, scraping his knees. But that hardly mattered to him. Jumping from the tram was a test of his courage.

Another test of courage was climbing to the very top of the Black Tower. The first time John met this challenge, he was terrified. He walked through the doors of the tower into its cool, dark interior. It was completely quiet inside, and he felt a spine-tingling chill run through his body as his eyes adjusted to the darkness. He moved toward the narrow staircase and held his breath as he hiked up the treacherous steps of the tower, climbing in complete darkness, feeling his way across a narrow ledge. Despite the cold dampness, he felt sweat trickling down his back. I can't turn back now, he thought, as he scaled a wooden ladder up to the open space on top of the tower. Finally he burst into the sunlight, his heart pounding, his eyes dazzled by the brightness. He clung to the stonework, his knees suddenly shaky, and gazed in all directions. The view was magnificent. It was absolutely worth the climb.

John's father owned a car, and on some Sundays John's mother would pack a picnic and the four of them would drive to nearby Klet Mountain. The hillsides were rich with deer, bears, wolves and foxes, as well as huge rocks. Legend had it that there had once been a massive castle on this high mountain, and that in it had lived, and ruled peacefully, the Duke Hrozen. The duke had only one daughter, the beautiful Krasava. Many boys wished to marry her – especially a handsome boy with a dark face and sparkling eyes, who was

The Freund family, (left to right) John, his mother, Erna, his father, Gustav, and his brother, Karel.

dangerous and devilish. When it was discovered that he actually was the Devil, the horrified Krasava rejected him, and he swore revenge. One day when everyone from the castle was away on a hunt, he created a terrible storm above Klet, which demolished the stone walls of the castle and littered the mountain with these great boulders.

It was there, close to the mountains, that John and his family spent their summers, in a farmer's house that they rented, near a village. It was a small but comfortable farmhouse with an old barn next to it. John walked in the forest and swam in the pond. He caught butterflies with his net and played with the village children. Those were sweet summers, full of joy and adventure, and Budejovice was a wonderful place in which to grow up. John could go anywhere and do just about anything. He had good friends, a loving family, and a happy home. He could not imagine that his life would ever change.

Chapter 2
The Neubauer Family

The synagogue of Budejovice was a large, beautiful red brick building located across the bridge over the River Malse, and set amid chestnut trees. It had two high steeples in front and two great Stars of David over its massive entrance. Inside there was a high ceiling and multicoloured stained-glass windows. Families sat in wooden pews, listening to Rabbi Ferda, who led the services from the front. Behind him, the ornately decorated ark held the torah scroll, dressed and adorned with a velvet mantle and silver crown. Rabbi Ferda had lived in Budejovice for years and knew everyone by name. The Jewish community looked to him for leadership and spiritual guidance. Still, at times the children found his sermons too long. With his loud, expressive voice and the stories he told, Rabbi Ferda tried to keep them interested in his services, and in their afternoon Hebrew classes. But he was not always successful.

I'm bored, thought John one day as he sat in the synagogue. It was the Jewish New Year, and most of the families of the Jewish community were packed into the synagogue. Rabbi Ferda's voice droned loudly from the front of the hall, echoing through the tall archways and bouncing off the ceiling and windows. John looked around, searching for a way out. He spotted his friend Beda Neubauer sitting with his family. Even though Beda was two years younger than John, they were good friends. Unlike the athletic and muscular John, Beda was small for his age, a delicate, clever and studious boy. Beda also had a great sense of humour. He kept John and his other friends laughing with his funny faces and the stories he made up.

Next to Beda sat his sister, Frances, and his brother, Reina. Frances was the middle child. She was petite and pretty, with a winning smile and shoulder-

John and his family attended this synagogue in Budejovice.
The Nazis blew it up on June 5, 1942.

length, curly brown hair that she wore in the latest style. Frances smoothed out the front of her red velvet dress and reached down to adjust her shiny black leather shoes. Reina squirmed next to her; he was three years older than Frances, but he was still her best playmate. Together they made puppets from rags, or chased each other around the chestnut tree across the street from their modest apartment.

Reina (left) and Frances (right), standing in the central square of Budejovice.

Beda and his family lived in a building at the entrance of the town – their home was right across the street from the train station, the point where people

Beda

arrived from other places. Chestnut trees lined the street, creating a thick umbrella of branches in the summer. Each autumn, the Neubauer children collected fallen chestnuts, adding sticks and material to fashion toy people. They even made tiny pieces of furniture from wooden matches and twigs. A table covered with a blanket became the stage for their 'chestnut theatre.'

Other times, the Neubauer children just sat on the stairs in front of their apartment, counting the cars that drove by. "I win!" Frances would shout. "I saw the brown car first! That makes ten cars for me, and only three for you." Spotting cars was their favourite competition. When they were bored with that game, they waited for the one-armed milkman, who came by every day with his cart full of aluminium milk cans pulled by a pair of large, ferocious-looking dogs.

Before Beda was born, Frances had begged for a sister. She had even left a note for the stork who brought babies, along with a cube of sugar as a bribe. Imagine her initial frustration when this baby boy arrived. "Send it back," Frances told her parents. "I want a baby girl!" But almost immediately she forgot her disappointment. Beda became 'her' baby. She loved to care for him, pushing his baby carriage under her mother's watchful eyes. Her precious dolls were neglected, left untouched in a corner of her bedroom, while Frances spent all of her time taking care of Beda. When Beda started to walk, Frances took him to the swings in the playground. They walked among the thick bushes and under the tall trees. They played in the sandpit and watched the puppet shows. Later, Frances taught Beda the alphabet, and how to read, before he even started school. "You're such a bright

Reina, Frances and Beda Neubauer

boy," she said, beaming with pleasure as Beda read his stories aloud.

Beda's father was an accountant and worked in an office close to their home. But he also worked as a travelling salesman to earn extra money for the family. He used his bicycle to get to his customers, but always reached home in time for dinner. Beda's mother was a talented knitter, and the family never lacked for warm mittens, scarves, hats and jumpers. She even sold some of her wares to shops to help with the family income.

The family loved nature walks. Each Sunday they would stroll through the nearby forest, where Mr. Neubauer would identify different birds from their distinctive whistles and chirps. The children would pick blueberries and wild strawberries. On the way back, they would pass the chocolate shop. The children found the smell of chocolate through the open windows irresistibly mouth-watering. Sometimes they were lucky enough to get a chocolate treat. For days after, they would remember the pleasure of the sweets.

In winter, the Neubauer children would go sledding on a small hill by the Jewish cemetery. Ski trails were abundant on the mountains and hillsides around the town. Wintertime was special for Frances for other reasons. Her birthday was in December, and Chanukah, the festival of lights celebrated by Jewish people, followed it. At Chanukah, her family would light their menorah – a candelabra with eight candles, one lit for every night of the eight days of Chanukah. The candles were lit from the master candle, which then took its own place at the centre of the menorah. Frances' mother would place their menorah between the double windows in the front of the apartment, where the children could see the reflection of the flickering flames. "Let's guess which one will be the first to go out, and which one will last the longest," Frances would say, as Reina and Beda pressed closer to watch the candles burn.

In the synagogue, John stared hard at Beda, straining to catch his eye. Finally, Beda looked up and spotted his friend. Together they nodded silently, agreeing to an unspoken plan. "Father," said John, in a soft whisper, "I'm just going outside to get some fresh air." His father nodded. "Don't be gone long," he said, and turned back to his prayer book as John stood to leave. Across the room, Beda was having a similar conversation with his father, who likewise nodded as Beda, Frances and Reina got up together and walked to the back of the synagogue.

Once outside, the children shouted at the top of their lungs, delighted to have escaped the boredom of the service.

"Let's go!" yelled John. "I'll race you to the park." And off they ran, across the road and into the park,

John and his friends played in this park across from the synagogue.

past the miniature mill, dodging under the draping branches of the huge oak trees. Passing the park benches and dashing along a gravel path, they finally emerged at the playground. The service was soon forgotten as they played hide-and-seek among trees filled with birds that flew as freely as the children played.

Chapter 3
A Proud Country

October 1937

One morning, John walked the two blocks to his school with his head down, wondering what the day would be like. His was a boys' school; there were no girls. And John was the only Jewish child in his class. That didn't bother him very much. Aside from Beda and a few others, most of John's friends were not Jewish. The children played easily together, not thinking about their religious differences.

John entered his classroom and looked around. His teacher was already at the blackboard, writing out the lessons for the day. He was a kind man who had taught John for several years. He nodded as John walked over to his desk and sat down on the narrow wooden bench. Three boys sat next to each other at each bench, with a long desktop in front of them. Zdenek was already there, busily writing down the lessons from the blackboard.

Zdenek Svec (pronounced Shvets) was John's good friend. They had known each other since they were five years old, having met and become instant friends in kindergarten. Zdenek lived with his parents and sister,

*Zdenek Svec lived in this school and played here
with John in the evenings.*

Mana, in a small apartment on the main floor of a
nearby secondary school, where his father was the
superintendent. As John slid over next to his friend,
Zdenek looked up and smiled.

"Come over this evening," he whispered, glancing
up to make sure the teacher did not hear.

John nodded. He loved going over to Zdenek's
home. Zdenek's family were kind, hard-working,
hospitable people. Zdenek's mother always had a plate
of delicious cakes ready for the hungry children
whenever John went over to play. And John loved
playing with Zdenek in the school. Together, the boys
walked through the dark corridors, chasing each other

21

John (front) and some of the other children from Budejovice.

and sliding on the polished floors. There was a rope-driven lift, mostly used for supplies and off-limits to the boys. Nevertheless, when they felt very brave, John and Zdenek ignored Mr. Svec's orders and took the lift between floors. "I have to go to my Hebrew class after school," John whispered back to Zdenek. "But I'll come over after that." Twice a week, John attended Hebrew classes led by Rabbi Ferda. The rabbi came to his school, and Jewish children from across town congregated for the one-hour session.

Zdenek frowned. He was not Jewish, and he didn't understand why John had to give up some of his playtime for religious studies. "Okay," he finally replied. "But come quickly after that."

John turned back to his studies. He had a long day ahead, and he needed to focus on his Latin, and on mathematics and history. But on that day the children were in for a treat.

The teacher turned from the blackboard to face the class. "Children," he said, "today is a very special day. Raise your hand if you know who Mr. Benes is." Everyone in the class shot up a hand. Edvard Benes (pronounced Ben-esh) was the President of Czechoslovakia. For years he had been Foreign Minister in the government of Thomas Masaryk, the country's much-revered first president. Upon Masaryk's retirement in 1935, Benes had assumed the leadership.

"Today, President Benes will be travelling through Budejovice. Our entire class will go outside to watch his motorcade pass through town. It will be an honour for all of us to see our president in person."

The class buzzed with excitement as the boys lined up and marched out of their classroom and out of the school. The streets were already jammed with people, young and old, waiting with anticipation. John scanned the crowd. He spotted Karel standing with a group of older children from his school, and he imagined that his parents were somewhere in the mass of people. In fact, all his friends were probably out here, waiting with the same excitement he felt. Beda, Frances, and Reina Neubauer were out there somewhere. Rabbi Ferda was likely standing with a group of people on another corner. Someone handed John the red, white, and blue flag of Czechoslovakia, and he waved it high above his head. And then, suddenly, there it was. A long, black, open-topped car rounded the corner, with a smiling president inside. Mr. Benes waved and nodded at all the people as they shouted greetings. Just as the car pulled close to John, the people around him began to sing the Czech national anthem, their voices rising in unison in tribute to their leader and their country. John, of course, joined in.

This was a proud day for the citizens of Budejovice. It was a day when vendors abandoned their stalls, businessmen left their offices, and mothers and babies lined up to get as close to the curbs as they could. John felt thrilled to be standing there waving his country's flag. He felt strongly Czech in that moment, and confident of his nation's unity. He believed that he and all the other people standing together were like one family, all proud of their country and their culture.

Chapter 4
The Nazis Arrive

March 15, 1939

On March 15, 1939 – less than eighteen months after seeing President Benes – John woke up to a grim new reality. On that day, hundreds of thousands of Nazi troops marched into towns and cities across Czechoslovakia, claiming the country as part of Germany, under the rule of their leader, Adolf Hitler. In Budejovice, some people were curious to see the soldiers. They came out to watch them enter the central square with their guns and their noisy tanks. But this was nothing like the day when these same people had been out waving flags and greeting their president. On this day, there were no flags and no happy greetings.

The Jewish families in Budejovice were terrified. Adolf Hitler and his Nazi party were known to hate Jewish people. Germany had been suffering terrible economic problems since being defeated in World War I, some twenty years before. A lot of Germans were out of work and struggling to provide for their families. Hitler blamed the Jews for many of Germany's financial difficulties, and in their desperation many people

*Adolf Hitler reviews his troops in Prague, Czechoslovakia
on the day of occupation, March 15, 1939.*

believed him, glad to have someone to hold responsible
for their worries. In the previous months, there had
been reports on the radio about hostility toward Jews in
Germany. "Something terrible is going to happen here,"
John's mother had said recently, as John listened in on
a worried late-night conversation.

"We'll fight against any occupation," his father
had replied.

John's mother laughed sadly. "How can we fight?
And with what? Our country is tiny, and no other
country will defend us. Hitler is a madman. We've
heard on the radio about synagogues being destroyed in
Germany, about people being turned out of their jobs.
And now I'm afraid it will be like that here."

"But our friends and neighbours will protect us if
something happens."

Erna Freund had sighed and looked away. She did not believe that anyone would come to their aid. There were some people in their town who, like Hitler, hated the Jews. They hated anyone who was different, or more accomplished, or owned more than they did. They would never defend the Jews of Budejovice. Besides, people were afraid of the Nazis and of Adolf Hitler. And fear could make people do dreadful things.

John had listened to these conversations, but he could not believe there was any danger, even as he saw his parents' troubled looks. Nothing was going to happen here in Czechoslovakia, he had thought. Not here in our hometown.

"You can't leave the house today," said John's mother, as the news of Hitler's arrival echoed over the radio.

"I want to see what's happening," protested John. "Everyone is out watching the troops. Even school has been cancelled."

But his parents refused to let him out of the house. John had no choice but to watch from his apartment window, straining to see what was happening outside. He could see the soldiers passing in tight regimental lines, wearing starched uniforms and high black boots. They marched with their legs straight up and down, their shiny boots cracking against the cobblestone pavement. Their arms were held out front in a stiff salute to Adolf Hitler. They were impressive and terrifying at the same time. How can this be? John wondered. How can all these soldiers simply march into my town and take it over?

A year earlier, Hitler had threatened to wage war in Europe unless a border area of Czechoslovakia, called Sudetenland (pronounced Sue-day-ten-land), was handed over to him. Czechoslovakia couldn't defend its territory alone – it was such a small country, compared to aggressive and powerful Germany. The leaders of Britain and France held a conference in Munich, Germany, on September 29, 1938 to discuss the problem. None of these countries wanted war. They believed that if they gave Sudetenland to Germany, Hitler would be satisfied. In exchange for Hitler's promise of peace, that area of Czechoslovakia was turned over to him, by an agreement known as the Munich Pact.

But Hitler did not keep his end of the bargain. He wanted more land and more power. In October 1938, President Benes had resigned and had gone into exile in England. And now Hitler had defied the Munich Pact, marching into Czechoslovakia and occupying the whole country.

For nine-year-old John and the other Jewish people in Budejovice, life changed almost immediately. Within a few days, a notice arrived on John's doorstep. "What does it say?" asked John, as his father brought the piece

Czechoslovakia in 1933 — before the war. John's town,
Budejovice, indicated by a black arrow, is located just below
Prague on the left side of the map.

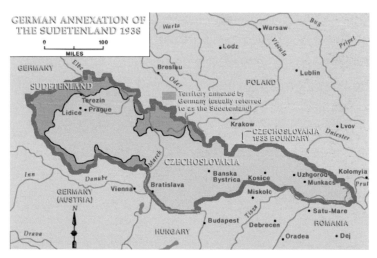

Czechoslovakia at the time of the Munich Pact. The dark area
surrounding Bohemia and Moravia, called Sudetenland, is given
to Germany in exchange for a promise of peace.

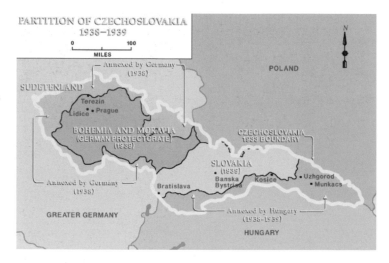

March 15, 1939. Adolf Hitler occupies Czechoslovakia.

of paper into their apartment. Gustav Freund glanced over at his wife and hesitated. "Tell me," insisted John. "I've heard Hitler's voice on the radio. I can see the soldiers on our streets. You can't hide anything from me."

"It's a list of new laws," began his father. "There will be many changes now."

"There are certain things Jewish families won't be able to do anymore," continued John's mother as she read the notice.

"Like what?" asked John.

"Well, we won't be able to shop in certain shops."

"You won't be able to go to the public swimming pool from now on," his father added.

John could not believe what he was hearing.

"Can I still go skating at the arena?"

His father sadly shook his head. "But you mustn't

worry, John," he said. "In a short time, everything will go back to the way it was. You'll see."

John nodded and tried not to think too much about the restrictions. He believed his parents. These new rules wouldn't last. How could they? He hoped that in a few days the soldiers would disappear, and so would all those new laws.

Instead, the rule of the Nazis became stronger each day. Swastikas, the insignia of the Nazi party, appeared on the fronts of buildings, warning Jews to stay away. These dark symbols had the power to exclude Jews from each and every place in town. Along with the swastikas came signs on stores and office buildings, declaring in bold, black German writing, "Juden eintrit verboten!" (Entry of Jews forbidden!) The park where John and his friends had played to escape from the synagogue services was now forbidden territory. All Jewish people had to be off the public streets by eight o'clock p.m. Musical instruments belonging to Jews had to be collected and turned over to the Nazi authorities. John's mother watched sadly as their beautiful piano was removed from their apartment. It left a big empty space in their home and an even emptier feeling in her heart.

John was able to stay in school until the end of that school year, June 1939. But after that date, Jewish children were no longer permitted to attend school. It was also against the law for John to play with his Christian friends. Children who had played with him in the past now kept their distance, afraid of the trouble it would cause their families if they were seen with a Jewish boy. How could they be good friends one day, and turn so cruel the next, wondered John, as one by one, his Christian friends deserted him.

Everyone except Zdenek Svec – the one Christian who was brave enough to remain John's friend even in the face of these terrible new laws. "Aren't you afraid to be seen with me?" John asked, as he and Zdenek played one evening in the dark hallway of the school where Zdenek lived.

Zdenek shrugged his shoulders. "We're friends," he said. "That's all that matters to me."

One day, John went out walking. He was careful about where he went, making sure there were no bullies around who might want to beat up a Jewish boy. These days, that was a danger. Across the street, he spotted his former teacher walking toward him. The teacher was a Christian who knew it was risky to speak to anyone Jewish, so John lowered his head as he passed. Suddenly the teacher stopped, blocking his path. John froze. What now, he wondered. But this teacher was not going to hurt him. The man looked around, reached out, grabbed John's hand, and said,

"Remember, you have to be brave." Then he quickly moved on.

John was stunned. Even talking to a Jewish person was a punishable crime. He felt grateful that this man took such a risk to be friendly to a Jewish child. If only there were others like Zdenek and the teacher, others who were still willing to be friends with a Jew. If there were, maybe things would be different.

The weeks and months dragged by slowly for John. There was nothing to do and so few places to go. He felt cooped up, spending most of his days in his room, or in the courtyard behind the apartment. He kicked his football against the wall and dreamed of an end to the restrictions. "When will I be able to go back to school, or play on the streets again?" he pleaded to his anxious parents. "You told me things would get better, but they are just getting worse." His parents turned away and would not look at him. They had no answers.

In Budejovice, as in other cities occupied by the Nazis, many Jews lost their jobs. To save money and help make ends meet, a lot of Jewish families gave up their large apartments and shared accommodations with one another. When John's father was forced to close his office and his medical practice, and was no longer permitted to work as a doctor, he invited a Jewish family to move in with them. He spent the hours

John's father worked as a gardener after being forbidden to practise medicine.

gardening for another Jewish family as a way to pass the time. But if anyone came to call with a medical problem, he was happy to offer his services. These new Nazi laws would not stop him from providing medical care to those who needed him.

In the meantime, the family continued to spend their savings. "How long can we live like this?" asked John's mother. She was worried that their money would run out and they would have nothing to live on. Luckily, Karel was able to help. He managed to get a job cleaning for two elderly people. It did not pay a lot, but the small amount of money he earned relieved some of the family's financial worries.

But everything else kept getting worse. Where would it end, John wondered. When would things go back to the way they had been? How much worse could it get? No one knew the answer. All they could do was wait and hope that life would soon return to the way it had been before the dreadful day when the Nazis marched in.

Chapter 5
Laws and Restrictions

July 1939

A new decree was announced in town. Jewish men were ordered to work on the banks of the Vltava River. Each spring, swollen from the winter's rain and snow, the river threatened to overflow and flood the town. The only way to control it was to dredge the bottom of the river, digging up sand and rocks, filling boats with this dirt and then piling it on the banks of the river to hold back the water. In the past, hired labourers had done this job. But now, more than one hundred Jewish men were ordered to take over the work. Among them was Beda's father. "How can the Nazis expect you to do this kind of manual labour?" Beda's mother asked. "You are an educated man."

"I'll be fine," Mr. Neubauer replied. "It will keep me busy, and make me strong. Besides, I'll earn a bit of money. And you know how much we need money."

His wife bit her lip but said no more. They were desperate for money now that he was no longer permitted to work. Besides, an order was an order. And so the very next day, at the crack of dawn, Beda's father and the other Jewish men reported to the river

Jewish men were ordered to do forced labour, in this case dredging the river to prevent flooding.

for their first day of hard labour. The work was filthy and backbreaking. Soft-skinned hands, unaccustomed to shovelling and hauling rocks, became blistered and callused. Often, men fell into the freezing water, fully clothed. Beda's father did not complain, but each night Beda and Frances watched as their mother tended to his cuts, sores and aching muscles. Still, they all knew it was the only way to earn money.

Before the Nazi occupation, Frances had been attending a German school in Budejovice. But it was hard being the only Jewish girl in a school full of Christians. For some time, she had felt the other children turning against her. They had whispered behind her back, pointed at her, and called her names. 'Dirty Jew,' some had jeered as they pushed and shoved her. Frances' parents finally moved her to a Czech school, where things were better. But by the summer of 1939, she too was forbidden to attend school. She consoled herself by teaching Beda at home, as she had when he was just a little boy.

One day, Beda, Frances and Reina made plans to go to the cinema. Finally we're doing something fun, thought Beda. "Be careful," his mother said as the children went out the door. "Stay together and talk to no one." It was becoming more dangerous for Jews to walk on the street these days, but the three young people hardly worried at all. They were going to see *Snow White and the Seven Dwarfs*, and they were too excited to think about danger. They sat in the balcony of the cinema and revelled in the bright colours of the animation, their eyes wide with pleasure and anticipation. The only entertainment at home was radio, and films with actors were in black and white. But this – this was magic.

The very next day, a notice appeared in the newspaper announcing that Jews were no longer permitted to go to the cinema.

Soon, Beda and his family were forced to change apartments. The Nazis wanted to use their building because of its desirable location across from the railway station, since German soldiers were regularly coming and going by train. The Neubauers moved into a smaller apartment that they shared with another family. It was cramped, and thirteen-year-old Frances hated sharing her space. Understanding this, her parents began to talk about sending her away to live with a family overseas. She would be safe there, and maybe she would even find a way to send money back home.

Frances at the age of fourteen.

In preparation for leaving, Frances had her passport photo taken, wearing a dark red dress with a stylish hat made by her aunt. But before she could go, a new law was passed. Jews could no longer leave the country. Frances' family scrambled to make other plans. They decided that, if Frances could no longer attend school, perhaps learning a trade would come in handy. "You're so interested in clothing and fashion," said her father. "You could help your Aunt Elsa in her dressmaking business. We'll send you to stay with her and learn the trade." He wrote to Aunt Elsa, who said she would be glad to have Frances come to her home in Brno, about two hundred kilometres from Budejovice.

"But she lives so far away," cried Frances. "I don't want to leave."

"Yes, it is a long way," agreed her father. "But you'll be safe there. You must go."

And so Frances sadly said goodbye to her family. At the railway station she held onto Beda. "Promise me you'll write," she said.

Beda nodded. He didn't trust himself to speak without crying.

"And promise you'll keep reading," Frances continued.

With that, she boarded the train. She had no plans for when she might come back, and no idea how long she would be gone.

Chapter 6
War in the World

September 1939

The Jewish families in Budejovice continued to feel the restrictions tightening around them, as the Nazi soldiers lived in their town and ruled it. One day in September 1939, John walked into the living room to find his parents huddled around the radio, their faces gloomy. John moved closer to hear the radio, and recognised the voice at once. It was Adolf Hitler, shouting out a proclamation to what sounded like a mass of cheering supporters. "What is he saying?" asked John.

"Hitler's armies have invaded Poland," his mother replied. "Britain and France will have to stop them now. There's going to be a war, a very big war." Her voice trembled as she glanced over at her husband.

Hitler's speech continued from the radio. "The Jews are our misfortune," he shrieked. "Workers of all classes and of all nations, recognise your common enemy."

John looked at his parents and he felt afraid. It was one thing to worry about the occupation of Czechoslovakia; that was scary enough. But they had hoped that Hitler would settle for the territory he now held – that things would not get worse, and would eventually get better. Now, the reports on the radio confirmed their worst fears. Hitler was trying to take over all of Europe, country by country.

Day after day, John and his family listened to the radio. Within one month of Germany invading Poland, the Polish army was defeated. The Nazis continued their push, moving against Denmark, Norway, Holland, Belgium, Luxembourg and France. And still Hitler pressed forward. As frightening as it was to hear about his victories, the Jewish families of Budejovice were hungry to know the truth about what was happening around them.

All across Europe, anti-Jewish activities were on the rise. As in Czechoslovakia, education was restricted for Jewish children, and adults were no longer permitted to own businesses or even work for their old employers. Like John's father, Jewish doctors, nurses, dentists and lawyers could no longer practise their professions. All Jews over the age of ten were ordered to wear yellow stars to mark them as outcasts. Jewish men were being taken away and forced to work for the Nazis, constructing buildings and railway tracks.

Still, John's parents tried to keep up a brave face. They didn't want to worry their children. But John was not fooled. Late one night, he left his bed and tiptoed into the living room. Once again his parents were huddled around the radio. Karel sat sullen and

Jewish men, removed from their former jobs,
are forced to do labour for the Nazis.

43

withdrawn in a chair. John bent closer so he could listen in on his parents' conversation.

"Jews are trying to escape from countries all across Europe. But it's becoming more and more difficult," John's mother said, as the radio boomed in the background.

"I can't imagine leaving our home," replied his father.

John's mother continued, "In Germany, all Jewish passports have been stamped with the letter 'J' to prevent Jews from leaving for Switzerland. Those who can afford it have tried to obtain illegal passports and smuggle themselves to safer countries. Some lucky families have managed to escape to freedom this way. But many have been caught and sent back to their homes, or immediately put in prison and punished."

"Well, we'll be safe as long as we all stay here," her husband assured her.

"These days, I'm not so sure. Perhaps we should think of escaping while we still have the chance. Many countries are not too eager to open up their borders to fleeing Jews. Just this past May, a ship called the S.S. St. Louis, with almost one thousand Jewish refugees on board, was turned away by both Cuba and the United States, and sent back to Europe. Who knows what will become of those families. We can't ignore what is happening."

"I'm not ignoring anything," sighed John's father.

"I just think that we can't rush into doing something extreme. I still believe we are safest here."

John watched his parents, feeling torn apart by the suspense. Would they decide to leave their home? Did they really believe it was too dangerous to stay? His mother looked so sad, while his father tried, as always, to remain cheerful. Finally they sat up in their chairs and shook their heads. It was not necessary to run, surely. It couldn't be.

Even so, John's parents were stirred to do something they thought might be in their sons' best interest. One night, they sat down with John and Karel to discuss the possibility of sending the boys away.

"It's impossible for your mother and me to leave our home," said their father. "But perhaps we should send you somewhere until the trouble passes. There are transports of children leaving Europe for England, to stay with families who are willing to take them in. It is called the 'Kindertransport'."

"It will be better for you if you leave with the other children," their mother added.

"But I don't want to leave," insisted John. "My friends are here, and you are here. I want to stay."

His parents lowered their eyes. They didn't want to send their young sons away, of course, but they desperately wanted to protect them. It was so hard to know the right thing to do. But before they could even begin to arrange for Karel and John to leave, the transports of children were stopped. The whole family was trapped, and surrounded by the war.

John was secretly relieved that he would not have to leave his home, and his friends and family. He and his parents never spoke about his leaving again.

Chapter 7
The Request

June 1940

Spring had arrived and John was restless. "What are we going to do all summer if we can't go swimming at the public pool and we can't go to the park?" he asked his parents. Like most people his age, John lived for the summer months and the chance to play outdoors in warm weather. The winter months had gone agonisingly slowly for all the Jewish children, with so little to do and nowhere to go.

"We must find a way for you and the other children to play together," his father agreed. The children needed a place where they could have fun without restrictions and without fear. They could no longer play on the streets or in the parks, and they needed each others' company during these difficult times. Jewish parents across Budejovice turned to the city's Jewish council for help in finding a playground.

The council was called the Kile (pronounced Key-leh), and it had always organised the social activities of the Jewish community in Budejovice. Kile comes from the Hebrew word *kehilot*, which means 'communities.'

After the arrival of the Nazis in 1939, the Kile had become the group responsible for carrying out the orders of the Nazis. In every occupied city or town, the Nazis encouraged a central Jewish authority; this was a good way to keep track of all the Jews. The Kile was forced to create a list of names of all Jewish people living in Budejovice, along with their properties and businesses. The Kile then enforced all the laws regarding curfews and job restrictions, and chose who would participate in the forced labour.

Sometimes, the Nazis appointed certain Jews to be on these councils. These were often prominent members of the Jewish community, people whom other Jewish families would be inclined to listen to. Many Jews refused to take part in these councils, believing that they would be betraying their own people if they carried out Nazi orders. Other Jews volunteered to be on these councils, hoping that, by doing so, they might improve the lives of their friends and family members, and delay or prevent conditions from worsening.

When the Jewish community wanted to ask the Nazis for some particular treatment or service, the request had to go through the Kile. So it was that in June 1940, the Budejovice Kile appealed to the Nazis for a summer playground for Jewish youth. Then they all held their breath, wondering if the request would be granted.

From his small farmhouse on the banks of the Vltava River, a farmer named Mr. Vorisek (pronounced Vor-ee-shek) heard about this request, and wanted to help. He was a kind man who had many Jewish business friends, and he hated seeing what was happening to the Jews in his town. Most important, he had some land by the river that was not being used. Despite the fact that it was dangerous to show any type of generosity to Jews, Mr. Vorisek came forward and offered his land – the swimming hole – to the city's Jewish youth.

The swimming hole, painted in 1941.

To everyone's amazement, the Nazis agreed to his offer. No one could believe that the playground had actually been approved. Perhaps the Nazis thought it was harmless for the children to have a playground of their own, or perhaps they believed that it would be a way to keep the children out of sight. Whatever their reasoning, the answer was yes.

The playground was a patch of land, right on the Vltava River, that was fifty metres wide and three hundred metres long. The swimming hole was located across a bridge, just outside the town limits. On the land was a rundown shack and nothing else. The area was not particularly attractive, and the river flowing past it was polluted, but the playground provided the children with a place to gather. It's just for us, thought John. There are no signs there to keep Jews out. It's a place where we can forget what is happening in our town and our country. The swimming hole was where the Jewish youth of Budejovice gathered for the first time in the summer of 1940.

On that first day, John climbed onto his bicycle and said goodbye to his parents. "I'll be back later today," he said. He couldn't wait to get to the playground.

"Be careful," his parents warned, reminding him that it was dangerous to be a Jew on the streets. But John didn't care. He was so excited to finally have a place to go. He rode his bike through Budejovice, across the bridge and toward the city limits. He arrived at the swimming hole, and who was the first person he saw? It was Beda, his good friend. Beda missed his sister, Frances, who had by now been away at Aunt Elsa's for some months. When he saw John, his face brightened. The boys happily greeted one another, and then looked around. About sixty girls and boys were already at the river, and more were arriving.

When John spotted Rita Holzer, his face turned a bright shade of red. John had a secret crush on Rita, a round-faced, curly-haired girl whose nickname was Tulina. (Tulina is Czech for 'cuddly.') She was a pretty girl with big, beautiful eyes and an infectious laugh. John was pleased that Tulina had come out to the

Tulina (Rita Holzer).

swimming hole. That would make things even more interesting. But he was too shy to talk to her, or to show that he liked her. Maybe he would get over that as time went on. For now, it was time to have fun.

One of the older boys suggested a game of football, the most popular sport in the area. The boys formed teams and a game began. John loved to play football; it was one of his favourite games. He ran with the ball, kicking it down the length of the grassy land in front of the river, dodging this way and that, trying to score. Other bigger and stronger players tried to push him out of the way, but that didn't stop him. On the sidelines, children cheered and jumped up and down. Maybe Tulina is watching me, thought John, as he ran and kicked the ball harder. By the time the game ended, everyone was exhausted but happy.

That same afternoon, Beda and John played a game of chess by the river, lazily moving their pieces around the chessboard and lying back to let the warm spring sun wash over them.

John looked over at his good friend. "Are you coming back tomorrow?" he asked.

Beda nodded. "There's no place I'd rather be."

Chapter 8
Summer Days at the Swimming Hole

July 1940

Day after day, John, Beda and the other children returned to the swimming hole, where they found their friends. They spent the warm days playing sports. Football was always the favourite, but volleyball was a close second. At weekends, even adults would come out to watch and play. By July, two table tennis tables had appeared on the playground. As long as it was not too windy, the children could play table tennis outdoors, smashing the balls with their well-worn paddles.

The balls from these sporting events often ended up in the waters of the Vltava. The river in this part of town was cold and the current was dangerous. But worse than that, the water was filthy. Raw sewage floated on the surface. Debates raged over who was going to retrieve a ball lost in the water – but not for too long, or the ball would disappear forever, swept away by the fast-flowing current. Eventually some brave person would wade out to rescue the ball and return it to shore, and the games would continue, only to stop again when the ball once more sailed into the river!

When it was very hot, the children went swimming. The first time John and Beda went for a swim, they held their breath and closed their eyes.

"Whatever you do," said Beda, "don't put your head underwater." John agreed wholeheartedly. The river stank. But the air was stifling hot, and even this foul water was inviting, so the boys waded in and dunked themselves. Some young people even had inner tubes, and lazily drifted by.

John always kept a lookout for Tulina. From the corner of his eye, he watched to see if she was looking his way. If she glanced at him, or smiled and waved, he was pleased.

Everyone had to pay to enter the playground, about ten Czech cents for a younger child, and twenty cents for older youth. Even though money was hard to come by, John's parents always gave him the change he needed to go to the swimming hole. The boy who took the money was the one who cleaned up the cabin and the whole area. He had been hired by the parents to keep an eye on things at the swimming hole, and he insisted on being paid for his services. "Ten cents," he ordered, as John and the others lined up to get inside.

"What if we don't pay you?" shouted one boy, who was pushing to get close to the front of the line.

"If you don't pay, I'll close the place up," the boy

*John (far left, wearing the bandana) and his friends
at the swimming hole.*

shouted back. "Everyone has to pay to get in." He did
not really have the authority to close the swimming
hole, but no one wanted to argue too much.

"I'll give you five cents," a young girl countered,
reaching into her pocket for the change.

"Ten cents, or you can forget about coming in."
That was the final word: everyone had to pay. And, like
it or not, they couldn't be in the swimming hole without
the boy. He was also the lifeguard. He swam out to
rescue the weaker swimmers, who were sometimes
pulled away by the strong undertow.

When the weather was bad, the old shack was the
place to go. It was run-down, with rotting boards that
creaked if the wind blew too hard, but it provided
much-needed protection from rain. There the children

sang and played indoor games. John and Beda's ongoing chess competition was fierce. Beda was quiet but very clever. Even though he was younger than John, he was the one who usually won at chess.

Each day, on the way to the swimming hole, John would look for the sweet vendor. The children called him old Mr. Papa, and his wagon was always full of sweets, apples and chocolate bars. He could be found in the shade of the large railway bridge, close to the swimming hole. Whenever he could afford it, John bought a chocolate ball from Mr. Papa. Children lined up to buy the treats, and those who had no money stood nearby, eagerly hoping for a bite from a generous friend.

At the end of every day, as evening approached, the children knew they had to get home. One by one they left the playground, reluctant to abandon their friends and their games. By seven o'clock, those on foot began their trek home. By seven-thirty, John and the others who rode bicycles knew that they had to leave as well. It was getting late, and the curfew would soon take effect; Jewish people caught on the street after eight o'clock were punished.

As John climbed onto his bicycle each evening, he looked back at the playground, and he knew he would return first thing the next day.

John and Karli Hirsch at the swimming hole.

Chapter 9
Ruda's Idea

August 1940

Like all the other Jews in the city, fifteen-year-old Ruda Stadler was frustrated by the rules eroding his freedom, more and more, day by day. He hated the laws and the Nazis who had written them. Most of all, he hated not being able to go to school. Ruda was a tall, strong and fit young man. He was talented and well-read. And he was clever.

"How can we just sit by and obey all these rules?" he asked his sister, Irena. She was only one year older. He could say things to her that he couldn't reveal to anyone else. "I want to stop this work I'm doing, and go back to school," he announced defiantly. When Ruda was forced to leave school, he had become an apprentice to a confectioner, learning to make sweets. It was nice to have sweet treats to bring home, but he didn't like his work. He wanted to be in school. He wanted to learn, and to use his mind.

Irena smiled at her brother. She admired his feistiness. "Ruda, you think too much," she said. "Why can't you just follow the rules and stop questioning everything?"

"But you hate what's happening as much as I do," countered Ruda. "Do you like the fact that we had to change apartments because our father isn't allowed to work?" Like the Neubauers and many others, the Stadlers had been forced to move out of their large flat to save money. They now lived in a single basement room.

Irena shook her head. "Do you like the work you do?" Ruda continued, confronting his sister. Irena was attending classes where – like Frances – she was learning dressmaking. But she hated the fact that a real education was being denied to her. Even though she was an excellent, creative seamstress, she could not take pleasure in her skill.

"You know I don't," she said, sighing. "I want to be back in school, just like you. I don't like anything that has happened to us and our friends. But there's nothing we can do about it."

That wasn't a good enough answer for Ruda. There had to be something he could do. He was not willing to give in to these endless new laws. He didn't like it when grown-ups told him to follow unfair rules that made no sense. He had to find a way to speak out. But how?

In the meantime, the summer playground at the swimming hole was a welcome retreat, a place for Ruda to relax and, at least for a short time, abandon his

A game of table tennis at the swimming hole. Ruda is the tall boy in the centre, wearing a bathing suit.

frustrations. Like the others, he had become a frequent visitor. As soon as he finished his work, he would head there. Volleyball was his favourite sport. He was good at it, and admired by all the other players. He was nicknamed 'Digger' because of the way he received a ball that was served to him. Placing his hands together at waist level, he would scoop or 'dig' the ball up from down low.

Meeting together every day, the young Jews of the city felt connected to one another. Ruda could see that, and he wanted to find a way for them to strengthen their bond, and feel even stronger. There must be more we can do here, he thought one day, as he lay in the sun close to the river. Behind him, the younger children

60

were playing a wild game of football, running from one end of the field to the other, shouting and shoving one another playfully. Playing sports is fine – but how long can we continue to just play, thought Ruda. We're brighter than that. We may not be able to go to school, but everyone here has a brain and should use it well. Besides, the warm summer days will soon end and it will be too cold to come here. Then what will we all do every day? How will we stay connected to each other?

And then, one day in August 1949, the answer came to him. Ruda had been a talented writer in school. Reading and writing stories had been the activities he enjoyed most. Writing would be the perfect way to continue to use his mind, to provide an outlet for his energy and creativity. But this time, he would write not only for himself. He would write for the other young people at the swimming hole. He would start a newspaper – a magazine that would prove that Jewish youth could do more than just play. He would encourage the community, especially the children, to band together and use their imaginations.

The next time he came to the playground, he brought an old typewriter from home. Luckily, it still worked. He also brought some paper. He took them into the old shack, and sat down and thought. First of all, he wanted to introduce the newspaper to the others and explain its purpose. He needed to convince them that there was a better way to spend their time.

He sat down at the typewriter and wrote this introduction:

Since we've exhausted every type of entertainment that can be done at our beautiful swimming area, I want to outline a few words about those who come every day, and add a few witty remarks about them.

Then he went to work, listing the names of all the young people who came to the swimming hole every day, and trying to think of something interesting to say about each one of them.

Karel Freund is the terror of the swimming hole. He shouts and threatens everyone.... We warn you not to ride a bicycle with him.

John Freund is better than his brother, Karel, though he is a menace to others; he prevented an accident on a nearby railroad bridge.

Anka Frenklova likes to eat, as demonstrated by her spreading waistline.

Irena Stadler has become like a mother to all the girls, both small and older....

The first edition of Klepy *was three pages long.* Ruda *listed the names of the young people who came out to the swimming hole and wrote something witty about each of them.*

63

Klepy *is Czech for 'gossip'. This drawing of a gossipy woman was on the cover of most editions.*

Dascha and Rita Holzer are faithful visitors to the swimming hole....

Herta Freed is a clever girl who knows many languages....

Suzu Kulkova is an easy-going girl whose heart belongs to Uli, the football player.... She is also an excellent rugby goalkeeper.

Ruda worked alone, telling no one what he was doing. He kept to himself, writing and thinking about his mission. He wondered if people would take it seriously. He even wondered if some people might be offended by his remarks about them. In his first editorial, he wrote:

This newspaper was created by Ruda Stadler. I'm the only one responsible for its content. If people don't like it, or are insulted, they should contact me.

I'll write one edition of the paper and see what happens, he thought. If no one likes it, I'll forget about doing any more. He gathered information like an investigative reporter, and compiled what he learned into three typed pages.

Next, he gave some thought to a name for the paper. He wanted to keep it light. Finally, he decided to call it *Klepy*, Czech for 'gossip.' It was the perfect title.

On August 30, 1940, Ruda produced the first edition of *Klepy*. He made only one copy. It was difficult enough to do that; it would be impossible to duplicate it. He decided that he would circulate the newspaper to all the young people at the swimming hole, and see what their reaction was.

A sign-off sheet accompanied the paper. When people finished reading *Klepy*, they were to sign their names on the sheet, add a comment or two, and pass the newspaper on to someone else. In this way, they would all have a chance to read Ruda's bold new experiment. As for Ruda, he could only sit and wait. Would they like his paper? Would they be irritated – or worse yet, bored? What would they say?

Chapter 10
Everyone loves Klepy

Ruda could not believe the excited response that greeted his little newspaper. All across the playground, young people were eager to get their hands on the paper and read what he had written. One child barely finished reading *Klepy* before the next child grabbed it. Not only did they love the newspaper, but they wanted more. "You have to produce another issue," Reina Neubauer said.

Ruda agreed. "I can't believe how popular these few pages are," he said. "But I'm so glad. I knew I could do more than play volleyball here." Writing that first edition of *Klepy* had been exciting, and he wanted to do more. But it was a lot of work, and he no longer wanted to do it alone. "If I'm going to produce another issue, I'll need help."

Ruda approached some of his friends – sixteen-year-old Rudi Furth and his fourteen-year-old brother, Jiri. Together they spoke with an older boy, Karli Hirsch. "With more people involved, we could really turn this into something important," Ruda said. "Not just a few pages of descriptions, but a real newspaper, with meaningful stories and articles." The other boys nodded eagerly. They wanted to be part of the newspaper as well. "Since I am the founder of the paper, I'll write the editorial," Ruda continued. "But what else should we include?"

The boys thought and thought. "Sports!" Jiri said. "The paper has to have a sports section. Sports are what brought us here in the first place. They are what keep us coming back day after day. Everyone would be interested in reading about the football matches here."

"Maybe poetry," added Karli. "We can write poems about the swimming hole, and what we love about being here."

"We don't want to make it too serious."

"That's right. There has to be some fun in the paper as well."

"And it has to appeal to everyone, young and old."

The discussion continued, with each boy adding his thoughts and ideas. Ruda listened, running a hand through his thick, curly hair. There was so much to do if they were going to produce an actual newspaper. But he was excited and his mind raced with new energy and enthusiasm.

On September 15, the second edition of *Klepy* came out. It began with an editorial by Ruda, describing in more detail what the playground and swimming hole meant to the Jewish youth of Budejovice. He wrote:

In the middle of the summer of 1940, permission was given to establish a Jewish swimming area. Hurrah for us; we have a place for recreation, sport and fun. Since June 16, we have been enjoying the Jewish playground.

He went on to explain some of the rules of the swimming hole, with a few tongue-in-cheek rules of his own.

If you are a boy, and you mistakenly enter the girls' changing cabin, you will be met by a storm of screeching girls. If a girl makes a mistake and enters the boys' cabin, she is welcomed with joy.

The original editorial team, (top to bottom) Ruda Stadler, Karli Hirsch, Rudi Furth, Jiri Furth.

That second edition also included a poem, encouraging the young people to find a way to continue their friendship and loyalty to one another as summer ended:

Our playground is so very nice,
With a cabin, small and fun.
But when winter comes and all is ice,
We'll have no place to come.
So, Jewish children, what we need,
Is a cabin close to town.
Where our fantasies, come true indeed.
With songs and play and joyous sound!

When Ruda circulated the second edition of *Klepy* the reaction was even better than the response to the first one. The children laughed at the silly jokes, enjoyed the poetry, and delighted in the sports articles. More than that, the adults in Budejovice wanted to read *Klepy* as well. It was not enough to pass the newspaper around the playground. Now it was going to be circulated to the entire Jewish community. *Klepy* had become a huge success.

Left: Ruda's editorial in the second edition of Klepy described the rules of the swimming hole. Right: The second edition of Klepy included a poem, which encouraged the young people to find ways to continue their friendship as the summer ended.

Chapter 11
Back to School

September 1940

As August gave way to September, and a third edition of *Klepy* was published, the children needed the newspaper's optimistic message of friendship and camaraderie more than ever. Adolf Hitler's power was increasing and his persecution of Jews was escalating. His armies were spreading across Europe, defeating country after country. At times, it appeared that nothing could slow the Nazis down. Each evening John listened to radio broadcasts with his parents, and the news kept getting worse. Italy and Japan had teamed up with Germany, and so had Hungary, Romania, and Slovakia. Denmark and Norway had been defeated. France, Belgium and Luxembourg had fallen, and so had the Netherlands. Britain was fighting back bravely against endless bombing raids. Canada, Australia and New Zealand were all taking Britain's side. But the United States was refusing to join the war.

John's parents received letters from family members in other countries. They talked about cities in Poland and Germany in which large sections were being blocked off. Jews were being ordered to move to these 'ghettos' – to leave their homes and belongings behind, and move into cramped apartments, often sharing tiny spaces with two or three other families. Food was scarce inside the ghettos. And even if food had been available, money was in yet shorter supply. Children and grown-ups became sick. The elderly were especially at risk. And each day, more and more Jews arrived from neighbouring towns and villages, and the crowding, the shortages and the health problems grew worse.

"How much longer can this go on?" John's mother asked one evening, as she listened to Czech-language news from Great Britain on the shortwave radio. The Czech radio station was in the hands of the Nazis, of course, but the British translated the news into all the languages of Europe, to tell people the truth, and reveal Hitler's lies.

John's father nodded. "The news from other countries isn't good. But at least we're all together here, and still in our own home, even if we do have to share it. Think of the families who have had to leave their homes in Poland and Germany, and move into the ghettos."

"That could never happen here, could it?" Mother asked. Father didn't answer. "But what about money?" she continued. "At this rate, our savings will be gone in no time. Then what will we live on?"

"We have to get used to eating less," he replied. "Less meat, and bread with no butter." He saw the look in his wife's eyes and added quickly, "Just for now. I'll work again soon. I'm sure of it."

John turned away. He hated to see his father out of work and his mother so unhappy. But he didn't want to think about war, and worse things happening in other countries. Surely there would never be ghettos in Budejovice! Even though certain places were forbidden to Jews, John could still walk on the street and play with his friends. Although the rules restricting Jewish families were increasing, the war didn't scare him. He was young and spirited, and he wanted to play sports with his friends. He even had a job to do every day.

His job was to deliver messages to the city's Jewish families. He rode his bicycle from home to home, leaving a notice with each household. The notice instructed the families to list all of their properties and belongings for the Nazi authorities. They were ordered to write everything down: how many rings, bracelets or pieces of silver they owned; how much land was theirs; the name and value of their business.

It had never occurred to John that, by collecting information about Jewish families, he was in fact helping the Nazis. "Don't you realise that you are helping to deliver this information into the hands of the enemy?" asked Beda one day, as John stopped by Beda's house.

The last thing John wanted was to collaborate with the enemy. But it was true that he had been told to do this work by the Kile, the Jewish council – and the Kile's orders came from the Nazis. Still, John had to continue his job. He tried to make the best of it. He even sang songs to himself as he rode door to door. But before long, his dilemma was over. His bicycle, like everything else, had to be turned over to the Nazis.

Now it was time for John and the other children to return to school. Autumn was approaching, and soon it would be too cold to go to the swimming hole. Even though normal school was forbidden to Jewish children, it was important for them to have some way to continue their education. And so, in September, they began classes with Mr. Frisch.

Joseph Frisch's family had a coal business in town. He was a talented young Jewish man who, in his spare time, played bass in the town orchestra. He was also studying to be a teacher. When school was no longer permitted for Jewish children in Budejovice, Mr. Frisch arranged for groups of children to come to his home for lessons.

The classes were small, only five to six children at a time. School started early, at about eight o'clock in the morning, and continued until about two o'clock in the afternoon. Children between the ages of eight and thirteen attended this school five days a week, and were taught by Mr. Frisch as well as some older boys and girls who were there to help.

Mr. Frisch was happy to have this opportunity to continue to teach. He had set up small desks in his living room so that the children could feel as if they were really in school. And the lessons were difficult. The children studied algebra, Latin, history and grammar. They had assignments to do after school and homework at weekends.

The first time John entered Mr. Frisch's home, he spotted Tulina sitting at another desk. At least having her here will make things more interesting, he thought. As he glanced around the room, he was happy to see Beda there as well.

There in Mr. Frisch's living room, the children were even able to continue their religious education. Rabbi Ferda came once a week to teach Hebrew and Jewish studies. Before the war, most of these young students had not received as much Jewish education as they were now receiving. There was no more hope of skipping classes.

Sometimes, Rabbi Ferda could be gloomy about the future. "Our fate through the ages is like a red thread of danger, weaving its way through time," he preached. Whatever did he mean by that, wondered John. Of course times were tough. But surely things would get better, and the war would end soon. I can't wait for that to happen, he thought. And I can't wait to

Mr. Joseph Frisch, the teacher (an image from Klepy*).*

get out of this class! Secretly, he longed for each day
to end.

Chapter 12
The Reporting Team

In those early autumn days of 1940, when John and his friends had returned to school, one of the few things they had to keep them connected was *Klepy*. The newspaper was doing what Ruda had hoped. It was serving as a link for the Jewish children of Budejovice, the one place where their thoughts and ideas could come together and be shared with everyone else. It was even more important now that they could no longer meet at the swimming hole. John and his friends read the stories from the newspaper aloud to one another, and then looked forward to the next edition.

On October 6, 1940, the fourth edition of the magazine was produced. By now, *Klepy* had a beautiful colour cover, drawn by a young artist who went by the name of Ramona. Ramona was really Karli Hirsch, who was now one of the editors, in charge of the drawings. His pictures were becoming a main feature of *Klepy*. Often, he took real photographs of young people in Budejovice, and added his own illustrations, transforming these photos into lively cartoons and comic strips. And how the magazine had grown! The fourth edition was eight pages long, and included a sports column, poetry, and detective stories.

The reporting team was also growing. Rudi and Jiri Furth had been part of the editorial group from the beginning. Reina Neubauer was beginning to write poems for the paper. Dascha Holzer, Tulina's sister, wrote stories, along with Suzie Kopperl. Suzie was the girlfriend of Karel Freund. She had already written several poems for *Klepy*, including one about Karel. Other writers, like Jan Flusser and Arnos Kulka, regularly contributed to the newspaper.

Ruda knew that *Klepy* was an important lifeline for the Jewish youth of Budcjovice, as well as the whole Jewish community. It was important to him personally as well. When he worked on *Klepy*, he could almost overcome the shadows over his life. But keeping it going week after week and month after month was hard work. He began each day by going to work at the sweet factory. Irena brought him lunch there, often rushing from her own work as a seamstress to bring food to her younger brother. When his workday ended, he met with Jiri, Karli, and the other writers to work on *Klepy*. They were very careful to finish their meetings before the curfew for Jews began at eight o'clock in the evening. But sometimes a few of them worked into the late hours of the night, and then sneaked home through the darkened streets, wary of the patrolling Nazi soldiers. Usually, they all met at Ruda's apartment to organise the newspaper. He had his typewriter and whatever paper and other supplies were available. When those ran out, they pooled the little money they had to buy more paper and pencils. Luckily, Jewish people were still able to shop in certain stores at certain times of the day.

"What are we going to write about this month?" Ruda asked his reporters, as they sat around the table in his family's small flat, planning the fifth edition. One bright light burned above their heads, casting dark shadows across their intent faces. Together they pored over the poems, drawings and jokes that had been submitted. Sometimes, they read the stories aloud to one another, eager for someone else's opinion, or unsure about exactly where to place the story. "These stories are fun," said Ruda thoughtfully, as he listened to Jiri Firth reading one. "But I think we need to write about serious issues as well." Ruda believed that, in addition to being entertaining, *Klepy* could also become a forum where important ideas were discussed.

"We must be careful," countered Reina Neubauer. "We don't want the Nazis to find out too much about us. If they think this is a political magazine, they might shut us down." Reina was a serious-minded young man who loved to write stories. Before the war began, he had often helped his sister with her writing assignments. As a result, Frances had often received high grades that she had not quite earned on her own.

The reporters looked over the articles for that

Clockwise from top left: Klepy *regularly included drawings, stories, a sports report, comics and a humour section. This sports column lists the ten rules of sportsmanship. The humour page has jokes about trains, and the comic strip also includes jokes and riddles. Bottom left: Karel Freund (left) and his girlfriend, Suzie Kopperl. The caption reads, 'You arc the only one in the world'.*

81

edition and sorted out their tasks. Ruda always wrote the editorial; that was his job as the creator of *Klepy.*

"We need another editorial that encourages people to write contributions for us," said Dascha Holzer. She was a bright, self-assured girl with a wild head of curly, brown hair.

Ruda nodded and sat down at the typewriter. "To all readers," he wrote. "Obviously your contributions have diminished. We understand that the swimming season is over. Therefore, interest in our paper may have gone down. However, we must keep *Klepy* going." He sat back, satisfied with his opening.

Tirelessly Ruda and his friends sifted through the many jokes and word puzzles that had been submitted, narrowing down the list of items that would appear in the next issue, in the humour section. Poems were also popular, so Ruda selected the ones that would complement this edition. Stories were next, along with a sports column. Now that it was autumn, and the sporting events had ended, the sports column was a popular reminder of warmer days.

The last step was to end the magazine on a high note. This was also Ruda's job. He was in charge of writing a section called 'Listarna' (editor's comments) at the end of every edition, in which he thanked those who had submitted stories and articles. He also added a comment or two about the various contributions. He knew it was important to thank everyone for writing.

In this editorial (Uvodem), *Ruda* appeals to readers to contribute articles to Klepy.

At the end of every edition, in a section called Listarna (editor's comments), Ruda thanked those who had contributed articles.

That was the only way to encourage others to submit their work. And more submissions were needed to keep the newspaper going.

There was so much to think about. They worked feverishly, choosing where the pictures would go and creating headings and captions. Finally, it was time to start typing. Ruda bent over the typewriter and pecked out the handwritten stories and articles. No one noticed the time passing as the pages were typed and retyped. Pictures were pasted in to enhance the stories. Each page had to be proofread several times. Ruda wanted no mistakes in *Klepy*.

Finally, Ruda stood up and smiled, and shook hands with his friends. They slapped each other on the back, hugged, and congratulated themselves. The fifth issue of *Klepy* was ready to be circulated.

Chapter 13
Ruda's Invitation

John left early one morning for Mr. Frisch's house. The skies were dark and menacing, and the clouds looked ready to explode with rain. Nothing was worse than a cold, rainy day that couldn't decide if it was autumn or winter and ended up being a mess of both, he thought. He pulled the collar of his jacket up around his neck. The jacket was old and fraying at the sleeves. It was a hand-me-down from Karel, but it was beginning to feel tight on John too. He picked up his pace. He would get soaked if he didn't hurry. Sure enough, the first icy drops were falling as he turned the corner to school. By the time he arrived at Mr. Frisch's home, it was pouring.

Inside, John caught Beda's eye and the two of them moved to desks in a corner of the living room. They pulled out their notebooks and waited for Mr. Frisch to begin his lesson. John yawned as the teacher's eyes gazed sternly in his direction. The day had barely started and he was already feeling restless. "Attention, students. Quiet, please." The class settled as Mr. Frisch began to speak. "Before we begin today, Ruda Stadler has asked if he might have a few moments to speak with you." With that, Mr. Frisch turned to Ruda, who had entered the living room and moved to stand at the front.

John brightened. He liked Ruda, and had always looked up to him because of his great skills in sports. Anyone who could smash a volleyball like Ruda was a hero in John's eyes. But these days, he was also in awe of Ruda because of *Klepy*. In fact, most of the city's Jewish families appreciated Ruda and his determination to keep *Klepy* going.

Ruda faced the children. "Raise your hand if you've read *Klepy*."

They all held up a hand, and some of the children snickered softly. What a silly question, thought John. Of course we've all read it.

"Raise your hand if you like what we've written so far."

Again, every child lifted a hand high. Even Mr. Frisch raised his hand. "The reason I'm here," continued Ruda, "is to appeal to each and every one of you to join our writing team. We can only keep *Klepy* going if each one of you in this room becomes a reporter. It's not enough to just read the newspaper. And it's not okay to read what someone else has written and sit back and criticise it. You have to write as well. We need more articles. If this newspaper is to continue to grow, then everyone has to become involved."

Ruda paused, allowing his words to sink in. John

glanced over at Beda, whose eyes were shining. Beda loved writing. This was the invitation he was looking for.

"What kind of articles do you need?" asked Tulina.

"Anything," Ruda replied. "Write something about your family or your pet. Write something about the swimming hole. Everyone loves to read about our playground. I know the newspaper was easier to produce during the summer, when we were all together. But now, more than ever, we need a way to stay connected. *Klepy* can help us do that.

"Every day," Ruda continued, "there are new rules about what we can and can't do. Well, the one thing that can't be restricted is our minds. No one can forbid us to think. So I'm asking you to use your minds and write something."

"Can we make drawings?" Beda asked.

Ruda nodded. "Of course. Draw pictures or cartoons. Write about people you like or people who are interesting to you." He looked over at John and Tulina, and John blushed furiously. It seemed that others knew about his crush on her. "Write jokes or comics. Bring all your articles to my home. I promise you, my editors and I will read everything you submit, no matter how long or short." He paused and moved closer to the students. "Think about seeing your name in print, and how it will make you feel. Ours is a small newspaper, but it can have a positive influence on our lives. I know that each

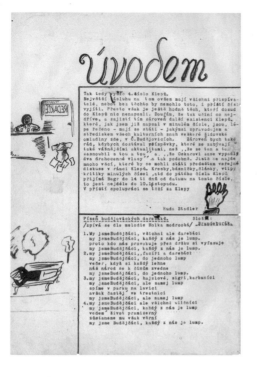

In this editorial Ruda asks for articles that are more serious. He writes, "So now Issue 4 of Klepy has been released. Most credit belongs to those who contribute, since without them there could not be an issue. However, many haven't written a line for Klepy. Now, I would also appreciate receiving contributions that deal with events that are more serious. Certainly one can come up with a lot of ideas that could become a subject for open discussion in Klepy."

of you has something to contribute – something important to say." With that, he thanked Mr. Frisch for allowing him to speak, and left the house.

The children buzzed with excitement. Several pulled out notebooks and began writing. Ruda had inspired them so much that they wasted no time getting started. As for John, his head was spinning. He wanted to write something too. Could he become a contributing reporter? He picked up his notebook, staring down at the blank page and imagining what his first contribution might be.

Chapter 14
A New Reporter

"It's here!" yelled John, bursting through the door of his apartment with another issue of *Klepy* in his hands.

"Wonderful!" his mother responded. "Let me have a look."

John shook his head. "I'm first," he said, and moved off into a corner where he could read the newspaper uninterrupted. This edition of *Klepy* contained his first article, and he wanted to look at it by himself. He thumbed through the pages, pausing to read some of the stories. His mother stood nearby impatiently, wanting her turn with the magazine. Finally, John turned a page and there it was.

How my father, a doctor, fixed my head

By John Freund, 10 years old

"Mum, please give me money. I need a haircut."

"You better go to Dad, son. He will give you some." So I went to see my father. He was sitting at a desk. "You know, these are bad times, and we don't have much money. As a doctor, I'm used to examining heads. I will cut your hair and shave your neck as well."

And so it began. Dad took the knife and began to shave the back of my neck. That was not bad. Then he took a pair of scissors and started to hack at me. You would not believe what a doctor can do ... "Ouch!" I cried out suddenly as my father cut into my ear. My mum, in the kitchen, heard the cry and came running. She opened the door and almost fainted. I had almost no hair left. I ran to the mirror. For a moment, I did not know whether to laugh or cry. My mother began to shout at my dad, until he gave in and handed me a coin for the barber.

When I entered the barbershop and took off my cap, the barber screamed, "What kind of artist cut your hair?"

Fortunately, the barber was able to fix what the doctor had destroyed!

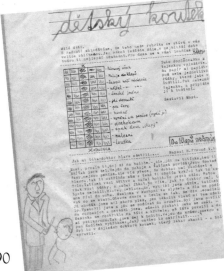

John's first article in Klepy, "How my father, a doctor, fixed my head."

John was thrilled to have become a contributing reporter for *Klepy*. He quickly turned to the back of the paper, to the sign-off sheet, to write in his name and his comments. He glanced down at the comments that were already there. Most people loved *Klepy*, and their comments were full of high praise. Some people had suggestions for what they wanted to see in the newspaper. Some even criticised the paper and its articles.

John took a pen and began to write: "First class. The newspaper gets better and better. Soon there will be one hundred pages, which is good. I can't wait for that to happen." Then he passed the newspaper to his parents so that they could have their chance to read it, and to record their comments. They laughed when they read the article about the haircut.

"I never knew you were such a wonderful writer," his mother said, proudly.

"How can I walk down the street after what you have written about me?" joked his father.

Any excuse to laugh felt good these days. Laughter was a way to forget the cruelties of the war, a way to feel that life was normal. Nothing else about life in Budejovice felt normal anymore. It was becoming increasingly dangerous to walk in the streets, and Jewish people were forbidden to enter certain parts of town at all. Arrests were becoming more commonplace, as Jews suddenly vanished off the streets. Where did these people go, John wondered, as his parents whispered about the disappearance of this acquaintance, or that colleague.

"Will we be arrested?" John asked. "Or crammed in some little shack?" he added, remembering what he had heard about the ghettos in Poland and Germany.

"No," his father said quickly. "We're safe here in our home."

When Ruda heard about these new arrests, he felt less certain about their safety. He believed that it was only a matter of time before the Jews in Budejovice were treated as badly as those in other cities. How could he believe otherwise? Since the first anti-Jewish laws had been proclaimed, the situation had kept getting worse.

All the same, he believed in the strength of his writing, and in the power that came from *Klepy*. As each edition of the newspaper was published, he continued to appeal to the young people to write more. And they did. They contributed articles, poems and drawings. Each edition was longer than the one before, and more elaborate. The newspaper grew from five pages to fifteen, and then to twenty-five. The young people wrote despite the restrictions placed on them, and despite any fears they might have. They wrote to reclaim their freedom. That was what Ruda had really done by creating this newspaper. He had pulled the Jewish community of Budejovice together, and given them something to fight for.

Chapter 15
Frances in Brno

February 1941

Far away, in Brno, Frances Neubauer was feeling very lonely and missing her family terribly. Aunt Elsa and her cousin Otto were wonderful and made her feel at home. But she was fourteen now, and she had already been away from home for more than six months. She had no idea how much longer she would be separated from her family.

Aunt Elsa lived with her son, Otto, in a comfortable apartment. Elsa's sister, Josie, a rather stern older woman who had never married, also lived in the house. Josie managed the household, preparing the meals and doing all the chores. She enjoyed this work, and the family loved her hearty cooking and her meticulous housework. Frances shared a bedroom with Elsa. Josie had a room of her own, as did Otto.

The Jews in Brno lived under restrictions similar to those in Budejovice. Frances could not go to school, to the cinema, to the synagogue or to the park. Her only friends were Jewish teenagers who had been introduced to her by her aunt. She was happy to have Otto's company – he was seventeen, the same age as Reina, and was a warm and fun companion. But she missed her family.

The only connection Frances had with her family was by post. The letters from her mother were full of descriptions of the changes in Budejovice. Her mother worried constantly about the war, and the impact it was having on Jewish families. But her letters also included wonderful news about *Klepy*, and the contributions that Frances' brothers were making to the newspaper. Reina had already written many poems and stories. Frances was not surprised to read copies of his pieces, but she was delighted that even Beda was writing stories for the newspaper. Reading the letters from home, she was filled with longing for her family. And she was envious. If she were still in Budejovice, she too might be writing for *Klepy*.

Meanwhile, Frances was becoming an accomplished seamstress. Aunt Elsa was a gifted seamstress whose skills were widely admired, and she still had a successful dressmaking business, despite the limitations on Jewish businesses in Brno. Her customers remained loyal to her, and continued to bring her work, while other Jewish businesses were being closed down. Aunt Elsa paid Frances, who was then able to send money back to her own family in Budejovice.

Each day, Frances sat at her aunt's side, in the

bright light of the living room, watching her create fashions for the customers who arrived on a regular basis. Aunt Elsa cut her own patterns, and taught Frances how to measure each woman and design a dress that would be unique and perfect. It was a challenging task, but Frances paid attention and learned quickly. The first outfit she sewed by herself was a beautiful peacock-blue dress with a white lace collar and fashionable pointy pockets. She proudly modelled the dress for her aunt, who praised her talent.

"I'm so proud of how much you are learning. Before long, you will be a fine dress designer," her aunt said, smoothing her carefully coiffed hair.

I wish my parents could see this, thought Frances sadly. She loved her aunt, and she was grateful for her generosity, but she longed to be back home.

One day, Frances went for a walk to buy a newspaper. She approached a park close to her aunt's apartment and paused. The park was off-limits to Jews, but it was such a long walk around the park to the stall where the newspapers were sold.

She shivered and looked around. No one was in sight. What harm will it do, she thought. No one will see me. And the park looked so inviting. It reminded her of the times she had spent with her brothers, playing in their own park close to the synagogue. The sun shone brightly, casting deep shadows on the path. The branches swayed in the cold air, almost beckoning her to enter. She took a deep breath and walked through the gates.

Immediately, Frances felt a sense of freedom and independence. She could smell the scent of pine cones, and imagined what the park would look like once winter had ended, and the flowers were in bloom. She stopped and bent to admire a small stream, with its glassy layer of thin ice, then straightened quickly and continued to walk. She couldn't dawdle, much as she wanted to savour this time.

As she rounded a turn deep inside the park, she suddenly froze in her tracks. Two soldiers in Nazi uniforms were walking toward her. Had they seen her? Yes – they had!

Frances' mind began to race, and her stomach lurched. What should she do? If she ran, it would make her look suspicious. There was only one thing to do – keep walking, and hope they would not notice anything wrong. As long as I act calm, they will never guess that I'm Jewish, she thought, struggling to compose herself. She bent her head and walked forward, trying to control the pounding in her chest. Ten more steps, and she would be past the soldiers. Five more steps, and she would be safe. But she couldn't help glancing up at the faces of the approaching soldiers. They were boys, not much older than she was. How is it possible, she wondered, for these young men to have turned against us just because of a difference in religion? They looked no different from Reina or Otto.

Now she was just steps away. I'm safe, she thought. I've made it, and I promise I will never, ever do this again. And then, just as she was about to pass the soldiers, one of them stepped in front of her, blocking her passage.

"What are you doing in the park?" he demanded fiercely.

Frances opened her mouth but nothing came out.

"Typical Jew," the other soldier scoffed. "She's too stupid to talk."

Frances felt hot and cold at once. How could they tell she was Jewish? She had no sign on her forehead. She had no banner announcing her religion.

"Get out of here!" the first soldier bellowed. "And don't come back."

Frances turned and she ran. She ran along the path, past the pond, around the tall trees and bushes, and out of the park gates. She ran and ran, and did not stop even when she reached her aunt's apartment building. She ran up the stairs, through the door, and collapsed in a heap on the floor.

"You were so lucky," Aunt Elsa cried, when Frances finally explained. "You might have been beaten or arrested. You mustn't walk in the street alone again. And never in the park."

Frances nodded. She did not need to be told. She knew she would never go near the park again. Before, all those rules and regulations had been official matters. Now – as she remembered the sneers on the soldiers' faces – it was personal. They hated her. They hated her family. But why?

Chapter 16
The Underground Reporters

March 1941

In Budejovice, as elsewhere in Europe, the radios blasted speeches from Adolf Hitler on a regular basis. Hitler proclaimed that the Jews were evil and had to be eliminated. Many German people were easily persuaded to follow this mesmerising leader, who promised wealth and better working opportunities during a difficult time – as long as the Jews were kept in their place. Besides, those who did not support Nazi policies were in danger of being arrested. Newspapers were also full of articles that blamed Jews for the war, for poverty, even for poor farming conditions. Citizens all over Europe were encouraged to turn against their Jewish neighbours and friends, or risk punishment themselves.

On the streets of Budejovice, Nazi soldiers were always on patrol, and they would arrest Jews for no reason if they were found in public. German enforcers were brought into town to keep the Jews in their place. These were big, burly men, thugs who took pleasure in beating up innocent Jewish citizens.

One day, John ventured several blocks away from his apartment, and closer to the centre of town. He knew it was dangerous to be this far from home. But he yearned for the freedom, for just a moment, he had had only a couple of years earlier – to walk wherever he wanted.

He turned a corner, going toward one of the cinemas. How long was it since he had been able to go to see a film? He looked up at the marquee to see what was playing and was quickly shocked back into reality. The cinema was advertising a new propaganda film that promoted discrimination against Jews. There was an ugly picture of a cowering Jewish man and a proud Nazi soldier standing next to him. John turned and ran all the way home. After that, he did not venture to go wandering again.

"The only place you are allowed to go is to Mr. Frisch's house for lessons in the winter, and over the bridge to the swimming hole in summer," his father said. "You'll be safe as long as you don't go near the centre of town."

There were new rumours now, about places in Europe where Jews were being arrested and sent away from their families, to prisons and work camps. Conditions there were brutal, and people were dying.

Ruda struggled with the growing rumours and dire

predictions from other countries. And most of all, he struggled for a way to write about these things in *Klepy*.

"We can't sit around, waiting for a future that may never arrive," he complained one day to the other reporters. The young people were gathered in Ruda's apartment, seated around the kitchen table. "No one is coming to help us. We must take responsibility for helping ourselves."

"What do you think we should do?" asked Reina Neubauer.

"Did you hear about Mr. Mayer?" asked Jiri Furth. Mr. Mayer owned the textile store in town, and had two children. "He was overheard criticising the Nazis. I heard that he was arrested and no one knows where he's been taken, not even his family."

Ruda sighed and nodded. The Nazis had forbidden anyone to speak out against their evil policies. They couldn't write in *Klepy* about Mr. Mayer's disappearance, for example, without risking punishment. It was one thing to produce a newspaper with funny stories and harmless jokes. No one outside the Jewish community cared much about that. But if they wrote articles of protest against the Nazis, or complained about their conditions, someone might report them.

"We'll be careful," agreed Ruda. "But we still have to say something significant." He wanted so much to speak out forcefully against their oppressors. Yet he knew that they had to keep a fine balance between entertainment and more important topics.

"I believe we can resist the Nazis with articles that talk about our strength and unity as Jews," he said. "Like this." He pointed to a poem in a previous edition of *Klepy*. Some time ago, Jewish men had been told to report to a central place in town, where they had been given shovels and ordered to clean the streets of snow. *Klepy* had published this poem about the work detail:

After a Snowstorm in January
Today the Jews went to work,
Looking strained, they cleared
the snow,...
Some were ashamed to be
seen.
Embrace your work,
So that we can show them our
strength!

Once doctors, accountants, teachers, and businessmen, these men were now cleaning streets. The poem was a reminder that they could still hold their heads high and work proudly.

"That's the balance I think we need to strive for," added Ruda. "One article can be funny and the next can be more thoughtful. One story can be lighthearted and the next can encourage community members to remain proud. Both sides of the picture are important."

"I agree with Ruda," said the outspoken Dascha Holzer. She had already written several passionate poems for *Klepy*. "The jokes are getting tiresome. Besides, how can we continue to tell jokes when people are being arrested? It's time to speak out."

"If we speak out as a united front, think of the power that will give us. Perhaps others will support us as well," continued Ruda.

"I disagree," argued Karli Hirsch. "We can't talk about resistance, or there won't be a newspaper at all, and our work will come to an end. We have to keep it light. That's what the community wants and needs right now." His drawings still entertained their readers, despite their growing worries.

"But don't you see?" exclaimed Reina Neubauer. "The paper itself is a form of resistance. It almost doesn't matter what we write. Just the fact that we produce it and circulate it is what's most important. That's what is keeping our community connected. If we get ourselves shut down by speaking out too much, all of that will be lost."

The reporters argued back and forth. Some were determined to keep the articles in *Klepy* carefree and humorous, saying that there were already too many reminders of the hard times they were all suffering. People needed to laugh and try to forget their troubles, not read about them in *Klepy*. Others, like Ruda, believed that the articles provided an opportunity to speak out more strongly against the Nazis and their oppressive rules. If it put them in some danger, that was a risk worth taking, to keep the newspaper meaningful.

There was no resolution to this argument. But one thing was certain – the world had become a dark place. And in Budejovice, one of the only things to look forward to was *Klepy*.

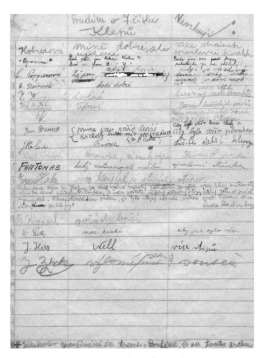

Every edition of Klepy *included a sign-off sheet asking readers to sign their name and comment on that edition. On this sheet John writes, "First class. The newspaper gets better and better. Soon there will be one hundred pages, which is good."*

Chapter 17
The Outing

June 1941

One warm day, Rabbi Ferda, who was in charge of school excursions, announced to Mr. Frisch's class that he was taking them to visit the viaduct where the rivers Vltava and Malse met. John was so happy. Outings like this were a highlight for him. The children enjoyed Rabbi Ferda's company, and besides, John and his friends would be able to skip school. It was much more fun to be outdoors than stuck inside learning Latin!

After lunch, they set off with Rabbi Ferda. For the most part, it was safer for the children to be away from town. The Nazis did not regularly patrol the rural areas. Besides, they felt freer in the country, away from the oppressive streets of Budejovice. Rabbi Ferda enjoyed being teacher and guide. On this day there was a lot of excitement in the group, and he had to work hard to keep the children moving. On the way, John and the others entertained themselves with silly jokes, tossing a ball and playfully shoving each other off the path. It was a long walk, and they didn't stop until they came to the pond. Some dropped wearily to the ground, but others decided to go exploring. They crawled in and out of the large plumbing pipes that carried river water to the town.

Once they arrived at the quarry, John and the others found a place to play football and do some boxing. Who could blame them for being excited? It was warm, and they could run and play freely for the first time in months.

John spotted Tulina playing with a group of girls. He wanted to be close to her and to talk to her. She was bright, funny and pretty. It was difficult for him to hide his crush on her. The others were beginning to notice, and sometimes that was embarrassing. An article about John and Tulina had even appeared in an issue of *Klepy*:

It was reported that last week John was seen climbing the stairs to the Holzers' flat, followed by several other boys. He wanted to tell his future mother-in-law that he was in love with Tulina. And you know, one of the other boys who accompanied John said that some boys had seen him kissing their younger daughter. Mrs. Holzer, although pleased that the son of the local pediatrician would be interested in the daughter of the poorest Jewish family in town, flew into a rage and threw the whole bunch of kids down the stairs.

It was a terrible lie! John really liked Tulina, and maybe he even dreamed about kissing her, but he had never yet kissed a girl. It was hard to face Tulina after that story was printed.

Now he mustered his courage and walked over to her. "Would you like to play a game of marbles with me?" he asked. Tulina nodded shyly. John sat down next to her and offered her the first large marble. She tossed it, trying to knock the smaller ones into a circle. John was impressed with her skill.

"Maybe we can play again some time," he said, when the game ended.

Tulina smiled and her dark eyes twinkled. "I'd like that," she said. John was more smitten than ever.

He returned to his own group, who were resting underneath a tall, budding chestnut tree. The sun blinked through the spreading branches as they swayed in the breeze. John felt as content as those branches, moving slowly to a springtime rhythm. He stretched his face up toward the blue sky and breathed in deeply. Then he looked over at the boys who were lying under the tree. Beda was there, of course, along with Rudi Goldsmith, a boy known as Goliath. The other two were Henry Kohn and Rudi Kopperl, boys of John's age who were also his good friends.

"Why can't we do this every day?" John asked. He loved these excursions with Rabbi Ferda and all his friends.

"The walk is so tiring," complained Beda. "I'd rather be at the swimming hole, or reading a book."

"I love the swimming hole too," said John. "But I also like being out in the fields." He rolled over to lie flat on his stomach. Underneath another tree, Tulina and a group of young girls lay talking and giggling. John stared at Tulina, watching as she pushed her brown curls away from her round, pretty face. She looked up and waved at him. He blushed and sat up to face his friends.

"What's the first thing you are going to do when we get back to the swimming hole?" asked Beda.

"Play football," replied John. He loved the days of running and playing along the water's edge. "And you?"

"I'm still going to be stuck doing errands. While the rest of you are playing table tennis and chess, I have to take meals to my father while he's working." Several boys nodded their heads silently. Now that it was spring, forced labour had begun again for many of the Jewish men in town, including Beda's father. These men were being made to dredge the river, to deepen it and avoid a springtime flood.

"I'm thinking of writing an article about it for *Klepy*," continued Beda. "I'll report on the working conditions of the men doing this horrible job."

In the distance, Rabbi Ferda called out to them, telling them they had ten more minutes to rest before

This photo/drawing of John kicking a football was on the cover of the fifteenth edition of Klepy. The caption says he is a sportsman who plays football and table tennis.

Beda's article, entitled, "Schoolboy's Lament." He writes, "Vacations are here. No more work. No more lessons. Free as birds. It's a magical time. That is what I thought. But instead of eating, drinking, reading, and going to the swimming hole, I have to take lunch to my father at his forced labour. My fate is bad. Life is like a ship full of misery."

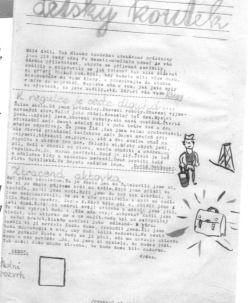

the walk back to their homes.

"Do you think the war will end soon?" asked Beda. Talk of forced labour had pushed his active mind into thoughts of the war. He knew from his own conversations with his family that Hitler's armies had recently attacked Russia. The war was continuing to grow. At the same time, maybe it would help that Russia, a powerful country, was now on Great Britain's side. He hoped so.

John shrugged. "I don't want to think about it." He didn't like to talk about the war, especially on this glorious day. There were reminders of war all the time. But today, he didn't want to think about the restrictions or curfews. As long as he had his friends and days like this, things couldn't be that bad.

"We have to swear we'll be friends forever," he said, to all the boys in the group.

"How long is forever?" asked Henry Kohn.

"It's until we're all grown up, until we're old," replied John.

"Let's promise to meet here in ten years," said Rudi Kopperl.

John nodded. "We'll meet at this same spot, under this same chestnut tree."

The boys agreed eagerly. "But it has to be more than just a promise," added John. "We have to write it down, like a contract, to show how serious we are about the pledge."

*The boys who wrote the blood contract, (left to right)
Beda Neubauer, Rudi Goldsmith, Rudi Kopperl,
Henry Kohn, John Freund.*

Beda pulled a piece of paper from his back pocket, along with a small pencil. First, he listed the names of the five of them: John, Henry, the two Rudis and himself. Then he wrote out an agreement vowing that they would all remain friends, and would return to this same spot in ten years' time. The boys passed the contract around and nodded their approval. But that still wasn't enough for John.

"Now we have to have a special ceremony, and swear we'll all follow the contract," he said. "And we have to sign the agreement in blood."

The boys solemnly agreed. This was an important moment for them, an opportunity to demonstrate how valuable their friendship was. In spite of the war and the sense of danger that surrounded them, they had to hold onto the hope and belief that they would be fine, that their friendship and their lives would endure. This oath would honour and unite that friendship.

They searched around the chestnut tree and found a sharp stick. One by one, they dug the stick into their hands, piercing a finger, and smearing a drop of blood onto the contract next to their names.

"There," said John, satisfied at last. "That part's done."

"But what are we going to do with it?" asked Beda, staring at the blood contract. "Which one of us has to take care of it?"

They decided to bury the contract underneath the chestnut tree, so that it would pull them back to this spot in the future. Once again they set to work, digging a hole underneath the tree. As they dug, one of the boys found an old metal box. It was a perfect container to preserve the contract. They placed the contract in the box, closed its lid, set it in the ground and covered it with soil. The contract was safe.

The boys stood staring down at the spot that they hoped would be their meeting place in ten years' time. They looked gravely at one another, shook hands, and returned to the rest of the group.

Chapter 18
Goodbye to the Swimming Hole

August 1941

One day, a new decree appeared in Budejovice. All Jewish citizens were ordered to wear a badge on their clothing with a yellow six-pointed Star of David. That way, they would easily be identified as Jews. Jews in other cities and countries had been forced to wear stars for some time. Some of them believed they should wear this symbol of their religion with pride.

But John did not feel proud to wear the star. He felt marked and branded by it. "We must do as we've been ordered," said his parents. "As long as we follow these rules, we will stay safe."

In Budejovice, Jews were now restricted to one small area. Though this was not a formal ghetto like those in Poland and Germany, the families knew that most streets and stores were forbidden to them. If they ventured too far they risked punishment or arrest. Much of the time, they stayed in their apartments, surrounded by their friends and family. Contact between Jews and Christians was prohibited. Zdenek

Svec, John's good friend from childhood, was the only Christian who refused to turn his back on John. Every now and then, John would sneak out to meet Zdenek. It was good to talk to his old friend. It reminded him of the days when everything had been normal.

Not long after that, John entered his kitchen to find his parents reading a sheet of paper. "What is it?" he asked. These days, orders arrived at the homes of Jewish families on a regular basis.

His father cleared his throat before speaking. "The Nazis have closed the swimming hole," he finally blurted. "I'm sorry, John," he added, seeing the shocked look on his son's face. "I'm afraid you and the other children will no longer be able to go there."

John could not believe what he was hearing. How could his playground, the place where he and his friends had enjoyed their best times, be off-limits to him? There would be no more chess tournaments and no more football games. He turned away from his parents. He began to understand, in a way he never had before, how the Nazis were closing in on them all.

One month later, even Mr. Frisch's classes were suspended.

The days felt endless for John. He wanted to be with his friends. From time to time, he was still able to get together with Beda and play chess or other indoor games. But there were no more tournaments by the swimming hole, and no more outings.

Chapter 19
The Last Days of Klepy

September 1941

In September 1941, the twentieth edition of *Klepy* was published. Though Ruda was proud that the magazine had reached this milestone, he was also very troubled.

Ruda always listened carefully when the adults around him talked. He listened to radio broadcasts and read newspaper reports whenever he could. His experience as a reporter had taught him to be a keen observer of details, to ask probing questions, and to read between the lines in order to determine the truth. From letters that other Jewish families had received, he knew about the ghettos in many European cities. There, food was in such short supply that people were starving to death. He could see how things were getting worse for Jews all over Europe.

"How long can we keep writing?" he asked Irena one day as they sat together. "How long can we pretend to be optimistic about the future when things get scarier day after day?"

Irena smiled sadly at her younger brother. He had always been sensitive and perceptive. His intuition had pushed him to think of a way to inspire the youth of

Budejovice through the creation of *Klepy*. That same intuition was now crashing down on him, making him feel more and more disheartened.

"I don't know if I can keep writing," he continued. "Each time I hear about prisons and work camps around Europe, I think it's only a matter of time before we are all sent away."

Klepy was the most meaningful task he had ever undertaken. It was a mission that had given his life purpose and focus. Ruda knew that he and the other reporters had achieved everything they had originally set out to do – *Klepy*'s reputation had gone far beyond Ruda's dreams. But now he felt he had completed his mission. He felt he could no longer write. It was time to step down as the editor.

He gathered his reporters together for a final meeting. "It's finished for me," he said. "I've written everything I can write."

At first, his team protested. "You can't stop, Ruda."

"Nobody can replace you."

"The work is too important."

Ruda agreed, but he said, "I've had enough. Besides, I've really done everything I set out to do. Look around. People feel proud of our community and proud to be Jewish. I believe that has a lot to do with our commitment to *Klepy*."

The boys and girls nodded. It was true that

there was a strong sense of pride within the Jewish community of Budejovice. The Nazis might have stripped away their property and belongings, but not who they were inside. *Klepy* had given people dignity in these terrible times.

"What will happen to the newspaper?" asked Reina Neubauer.

"Maybe someone else wants to take it over," suggested Ruda. "I'm happy for anyone to do that, if they want."

That evening, Ruda sat down to write his final editorial. In it, he returned to the original purpose of *Klepy*: "To give expression to the pride of the Jewish youth of our town; to energise them to physical and mental achievements.... For two summers we have played sport, established friendships, and kept up our spirit." He ended his editorial by saying, "We hope to meet you again...."

Ruda's comments were strong but a bit sad – as if he wasn't sure that there would be a future for *Klepy* or for its creators. All across town, people read the editorial and felt desolate and uncertain.

When the winter of 1941 arrived, there were two more issues of *Klepy*. Milos Konig, a young boy who had written articles for the newspaper, took Ruda up on his challenge to keep it going. He became the editor for these last two issues. But they were not the same as the old *Klepy*. There were fewer jokes, and the articles were more serious as they looked back at past pleasures and worried about the future. There were wistful poems about memories of the swimming hole, and solemn proverbs that reminded families about sacrifice.

Reina arrived at Ruda's home to drop off the final edition. "We can't do it anymore," he said. "It's no longer safe for us to meet, and it's impossible to gather information for articles. We can't even buy supplies. On behalf of all the reporters of *Klepy*, I'm bringing the last edition to you."

Ruda took the copy from Reina's hands with a sinking heart. He missed working on the newspaper. He missed being its leader and editor. But most of all, he missed the freedom it had represented.

"If anything happens to us, this collection must stay together," Reina continued. "We're trusting you to find a way to do that."

Ruda nodded, shook hands with Reina and closed the door. He looked down at the last edition of his treasured newspaper. Then he moved to the kitchen table, reached underneath it, picked up the box that held the entire collection of *Klepy*, and reverently placed the last edition on the top of the pile.

Top left: The cover of the twentieth edition, with the original editorial team. Ruda is in the middle, with Rudi Furth (top center) and Jiri Furth (top right). The missing photo (top left) is that of Karli Hirsch. Top right: In the twentieth edition of Klepy, Ruda steps down as editor and encourages everyone to keep their spirits high. Bottom: Photo/drawings from the twentieth edition of Klepy.

Chapter 20
Deportation

November 1941

By the autumn of 1941, Adolf Hitler had finalised his plan to kill all Jewish people in Europe. This plan was called 'The Final Solution'. Concentration camps were set up across Germany and Poland. These 'camps' were actually prisons built for the specific purpose of killing as many Jews as possible, as quickly as possible. Six of them would become primary killing sites: Auschwitz,

The Star of David that all Jews were forced to wear.

Majdanek, Belzak, Sobibor, Treblinka and Chelmno. As hostility toward Jews intensified, more ghettos were formed in towns and cities. These became collection centres where Jews were held until they could be deported to the concentration camps. Up until then, the Jewish families of Budejovice had heard rumours of these deportations, but only from distant places. But now, in nearby cities and towns, families were being arrested and sent away. Frances Neubuuer heard about this from her aunt's home in Brno, where Jews were already being deported. If her aunt was sent away, Frances would likely be sent with her. It would be better if she went home to her family. Just before her fifteenth birthday, in November 1941, Frances boarded a train to return to Budejovice. She came home in the last car of the train, the one set aside for Jewish passengers. She had not seen her parents, or Beda and Reina, in over a year.

When her father saw her for the first time, he smiled lovingly and sadly. "I sent away a girl, and you've returned as a young lady," he said as he hugged and kissed his daughter. There was no way they could make themselves safe. But if anything was going to happen to them, at least they were together.

To save money, the Neubauers had moved to a small apartment that they shared with two other Jewish families – a total of eleven people were now living in one crowded space. The only toilet was in the hallway.

In the kitchen, the women fought constantly about what to cook and how to prepare it. In the end there was not much to fight about, since there was so little food to begin with.

On December 7, 1941, the war took a dramatic turn. Japan attacked the fleet of American warships in Pearl Harbor, in the United States. Japan was a strong ally of Germany, and Japanese leaders thought that if they destroyed the U.S. fleet, they would be able to expand their empire into Pacific territories. It was a serious mistake. On December 11, 1941, the outraged United States declared war on Japan, and then on Germany as well. Without the power of the United States, Britain and her allies had been suffering terrible losses, and it had seemed all too likely that Hitler would rule the entire European continent, including Great Britain. Over the next few months, though, the balance of power would finally begin to shift away from Germany, and toward the United States and her new allies.

But it would take time to change the tide of war and turn back the German troops. In the meantime, all across Europe, Jews continued to lose their lives at the hands of the Nazis.

In early February 1942, all the Jewish families in Budejovice received the news they were dreading most. They were to be transported away from their homes. Their destination was a place called Theresienstadt.

Chapter 21
Getting Ready to Leave

February 1942

Terezin is a small town about sixty kilometres northwest of Prague, the capital city of Czechoslovakia. In 1780, Emperor Joseph II built a fortress there that he named after his mother, Maria Theresa. The fortress was built to protect the town from invaders. But in 1939 German troops occupied this part of Czechoslovakia, and in 1941 Terezin became Theresienstadt, a concentration camp.

When John and his family first learned that they were being sent to Theresienstadt, they hoped that living conditions there would be decent, and that they would soon be able to return home. "The Allied forces are getting the upper hand, and the Germans are starting to lose. In three months, the war will be over," said John's father optimistically. "Besides," he added, "Theresienstadt is not that far away, and at least it is here in our own country." Somehow, that was a reassuring notion. As long as they were not leaving their homeland, things could not be all that bad.

When the Nazis first established Theresienstadt as a

concentration camp, they had several plans. The camp was meant to hold prominent Jews of Czechoslovakia, as well as some from Germany and other western European countries. For many prisoners, Theresienstadt would be a temporary location. From there, they would be sent to concentration camps in the east.

Theresienstadt was disguised as a 'model' Jewish community. This meant that people were fooled into believing that Jews would be treated well there, that they would be given housing, adequate food and proper medical care. Supposedly they would be kept there for their own protection, and they would be given work. These lies were meant to convince people that the Nazis were treating Jews decently. In reality, the conditions in Theresienstadt were terrible, and the ultimate Nazi plan was for all the prisoners to be sent on to death camps in the east.

Of course, the Jewish families of Budejovice were not aware of this plan. They knew people were being deported to the east. They had heard rumours of horrible living conditions and death camps. But they believed that Theresienstadt was the exception. They hoped and prayed that they were going to a place that would keep them safe until the war was over.

John tried to think of the move to Theresienstadt as a new adventure. Things were so boring in Budejovice. Without the swimming hole and *Klepy*, there was nothing to do and nowhere to gather with his friends.

"Will I see Beda in Theresienstadt?" he asked his mother.

"Probably," she replied. "All the Jewish families are going."

Not far away, Beda and his family were also preparing for the move to Theresienstadt. Frances wrote a letter to her cousin Otto, who still lived in Brno.

Yesterday we received our transportation numbers. Mine is 391. Beda's is 392, Mother's 393, Reina's 394, and Father's 395. Uncle Moritz is 361 and Aunt Olga 362. On Tuesday, we will go to the Kohn frame factory. We are all packing now. I am baking some cookies. Do not grieve. I don't care. We hope it is all for just a short time. And then we will all meet again....

The most difficult part of the move was trying to work out what to take. Each person was allowed only fifty kilograms of luggage, which was not very much. Should they take summer or winter clothing? What about books, favourite toys, photo albums or food?

"What will happen to all our things that are left behind?" worried John's mother.

Despite the dangers, Zdenek Svec had remained friendly with John through all this time. Now Zdenek's family reached out to help. John's mother gave her fur coat, some artwork and several expensive rugs to the Svec family, for safekeeping.

"We will hide your things for you," promised Zdenek's mother. "They will be here waiting for you when you return. I hope it's not long. God bless and keep you."

Reina Neubauer wrote this uplifting poem entitled "The Joke" to make his friends smile despite their sadness. One verse reads,

So people, down with sadness!
Long lives the King of Joke.
As long as we all can laugh,
It is easier to cope.

Chapter 22
Hiding Klepy

Ruda Stadler was also wondering about what to take to Theresienstadt. He stared at the box of newspapers: twenty-two editions of *Klepy*, along with twenty-two sign off sheets. He thumbed through the box of papers and picked up the very first edition, three simple pages of chitchat. He marvelled at how the magazine had grown and developed in two years: from three pages to as many as thirty pages; from childish gossip to mature articles and drawings, jokes and poems. His editorials were there, along with the articles written by so many Jewish children of Budejovice. They had been underground reporters, and he had been their leader.

"Do you believe we really did this?" he asked his sister, Irena, when she entered his room. "Every day for the past two years, we've been told that we can't do this or that, we can't go here and there. And yet we managed to create something so special."

"You're the one who did it," Irena replied proudly.

"No," insisted Ruda, "everyone contributed. *Klepy* belongs to all of us." He picked up the box of newspapers. It was heavy.

"What are we going to do with these while we're

away?" he asked, remembering his pledge to keep the newspapers safe.

"We could take them with us," she suggested.

Ruda shook his head. "No, I don't think that's a good idea." The newspapers were heavy and he needed the space in his suitcase for clothing and other supplies.

"Maybe you could divide them up," she continued. "Give a few issues each to some of the reporters. I'm not sure keeping the collection together is the best idea."

Ruda thought about that, but then shook his head again. "No. Whatever happens to us, I believe the collection should stay together. Somehow, that feels like the right thing to do." He paused. "We're going to have to find a place to leave these while we're away."

"There's no place to hide them in our apartment. And we can't leave them here in the open," she said. "We don't know what will happen to the things in our home while we're gone."

"I wish I could take them with me," sighed Ruda. "But I know that's impossible." He paced through the small apartment. "Where can we leave the newspapers so they will be safe? Who can we trust to hide them?"

Ruda and Irena finally came up with a plan. Their former housekeeper, a Christian woman named Thereza, had remained a friend, even after it became illegal for her to work for a Jewish family. She had left the Stadlers tearfully, promising to assist them in the future. The time had come to ask for help. Leaving the magazines with her was the only solution. Ruda trusted her to keep *Klepy* safe.

He gathered up the newspapers into a big bundle and left his home. He ran quickly through the streets of Budejovice, careful to avoid any soldiers who might be out on patrol, ducking in and around buildings to avoid being seen. Finally he arrived at Thereza's home, anxious and out of breath.

When she saw Ruda at the door, Thereza pulled him quickly into her home, glancing around nervously to see if anyone had noticed him. It was dangerous for her to be seen with a Jewish boy, and even more dangerous to be hiding this Jewish newspaper. But when Ruda explained what he needed her to do, she did not hesitate. "I'll hide them, Ruda," she promised. "No one will find them in my home. And they'll be here waiting for you when you return."

"I'm so grateful," Ruda whispered. Thereza shook her head. "It's the least I can do for a friendship that has lasted so many years."

"I'll come back for them," Ruda promised, as he handed over the bundle of newspapers – two years' worth of work, imagination and resourcefulness. He felt as though he was handing over his past, his life. As much as he wanted to believe that he would come back home, he was deeply uncertain about his future. Even as he vowed to return, his voice was shaky, and he felt sad and empty as he walked away.

Covers from several editions of Klepy.

Chapter 23
Leaving Home

April 1942

"Wake up!" John's mother called from the kitchen. "It's late, and we have to leave."

John rolled over, stretched, and sat up in bed. His eyes moved around the room, finally coming to rest on the suitcase by his bedroom door. It was Tuesday, April 14, 1942 – the day he and his family, along with all the other Jewish families of Budejovice, were being forced to leave their homes and go to Theresienstadt.

No one spoke much at breakfast. John's father looked sad and withdrawn, as if he had no more answers. John's mother moved around the kitchen, packing up rolls and cheese and whatever bits of food were left in the house. As long as she kept busy, she would not have to think too much about what lay ahead. They all finished breakfast, and then John went back to his bedroom to complete his packing. His football rested in a corner of the room, along with his table tennis paddle. How he longed to take these toys with him! But these and other prized possessions would have to be left behind.

Where will I sleep, he wondered, as he made his

bed for the last time. What will I do all day long? Will I be with my parents? Will I be near my friends? What will I eat? What if I get sick? Will my mother be there to look after me? So many questions swirled inside his head. He worried about what would happen to all the things left behind in his room. He wondered when he would come home. He worried about what new rules and regulations would face him in Theresienstadt. And for every worry, there was simply no answer.

He finished dressing, and placed one last jumper into his suitcase. He took a deep breath and glanced around his room one last time. Then, along with his parents and his brother, he walked out of his home.

As they walked through the quiet streets of Budejovice, John glanced up at the homes in his neighbourhood. Most of the blinds were drawn, as if the Christian families did not want to see what was happening to their Jewish neighbours. John wondered how many of these families were happy to see the Jews leaving, and how many were distressed and fearful themselves, not knowing what they could do to help.

The first stop for the Jewish families was a small house in town, where everyone had to register, identifying themselves by the transport numbers that had already been given to them. The lines were long, but they all waited patiently for their turn to sign their names and list their numbers. From there they were taken to a large warehouse, a two-story wooden building that had been a factory once owned by a Jewish family. The wooden floor was dirty, but that did not stop families from staking out their spaces and dropping wearily to the floor. A few old mattresses were scattered about, but for the most part they slept on luggage and on each other.

The warehouse filled up quickly, until it was crowded and noisy. John was reassured to see many of his friends. There was Beda, along with Frances and Reina. Ruda Stadler was there, along with Irena. Rabbi Ferda walked around talking quietly to people, comforting those who were frightened. Even John's teacher, Joseph Frisch, sat on his suitcase, reading. Things couldn't be so bad if everyone was still together, thought John, comforting himself.

John and the others moved around the factory, talking to friends and relatives. And then, the children did what they always did when they were together. They played tag, and ran noisily in and around the people who were sleeping on the floor. They even got to go outside, into the yard behind the factory, where they wrestled and shoved each other good-naturedly.

After playing with his friends for a while, John joined his family, huddled on the floor.

"Here," said his mother, handing him a roll. "Eat this. We don't know when we are leaving and we must keep up our strength." They ate what little food they had managed to bring with them. Then the Nazi guards brought some soup into the warehouse, and shouted for them all to line up to be fed. The soup was thin, and not very appetising.

"What do you think will happen when we get to Theresienstadt?" John asked Beda, as the two of them sat together in a corner.

Beda shrugged. "I don't know. What do your parents say?"

"Not much. They keep saying the war will be over soon. But they've been saying that forever."

"Do you think we're going to come home again?" asked Beda.

"Of course we will!" John declared, pretending confidence.

At one point, all the families were ordered to assemble downstairs in the yard in order to be counted. They left their belongings in piles on the floor and moved slowly outside. There they assembled in groups, according to their transport numbers, and waited anxiously as the guards moved about, counting people and checking their numbers against the transport sheets they held in their hands. It took forever to count a thousand people. Finally, they were permitted to go back to the warehouse and find their spots once more.

As they returned to their luggage, John saw Tulina sitting alone in one corner of the warehouse. She looked scared, and John longed to comfort her. When he walked toward her, she looked up and brightened.

"I'm so glad to see you," she said.

John nodded. "Me too."

There was an awkward pause.

"Do you know how long we'll be here?" she asked. Her dark eyes were sad. Gone was her bright, lovely smile.

"A few days, I think. And then we'll get on the trains. Don't worry," he added. "We'll be fine." Once again, he sounded braver than he felt.

Tulina smiled, grateful for his encouragement.

"I'll just sit here with you," he said. "We can talk, or play a game."

Tulina nodded again, and they sat together in the warehouse, saying little, thankful for each other's company.

On the fourth day – Saturday, April 18 – everyone went outside to be counted again. But this time they did not return to the warehouse.

"Move along the railroad tracks," the guards barked. "Take your belongings and board the train." Everyone scrambled to get seats on the train, anxious to stay together as families.

The crowded railroad cars became hot and noisy. The doors closed with a bang and at last the train pulled out of the station, leaving Budejovice behind. John kept his eyes glued to the window as his town became smaller and smaller, and finally disappeared. When will I see Budejovice again? he wondered.

Chapter 24
Theresienstadt

April 1942

When the train pulled into Theresienstadt, John and the others had their first taste of what to expect. Fierce guards surrounded them, bellowing orders as the Jews descended from the train and assembled on the platform. "Move ahead!" the guards shouted, kicking and pushing anyone who moved too slowly. They all quickly fell into line, trying to avoid this abuse. Then they were marched toward a warehouse, to await further orders.

Theresienstadt was a dirty, barren town consisting mainly of three-story brick buildings, much like the apartment buildings in Budejovice, but run-down. Other, smaller houses stood between the taller buildings. These buildings surrounded a large fenced square, a muddy wasteland in the centre of town. A high wall patrolled by the guards enclosed the entire town.

The town was packed with Jewish prisoners from all over Czechoslovakia and other parts of Europe. Men, women and children shuffled through the streets with their heads down, dressed in rags, moving silently. Soldiers patrolled the small cobblestone streets, brandishing rifles. Guard dogs strained at their leashes and barked ferociously as the prisoners walked by.

In the dark warehouse, families searched for a corner where they might have some space and privacy. But the warehouse quickly became crowded, and people had to lie pressed closely against each other. John slept little that night. He lay with his head close to his father's back, his mind racing. There was a desperate feeling in the air. He could sense it in the strained faces of the adults around him. He could see it in the grimness on the streets and in the buildings, in the guards who patrolled nearby. And he could feel it in the hunger pangs that were already gnawing at his stomach. He moved closer to his father for comfort.

The central square in the town of Terezin today.

The next day, they had to line up outside to be counted again. John was exhausted, and stood timidly in line, wondering if they would be given a real place to sleep and when they would receive some food. The count seemed endless, but eventually the guards reached the families of Budejovice.

"Get into lines!" they shouted harshly. "Men on the left, women to the right, and children in a separate line over here."

John's heart beat wildly as this news settled in on him. Families were to be separated! Women were being sent to one large barracks, men to another, and boys and girls to two other barracks. There was mass confusion as parents all around him clutched their sobbing children. John had never been away from his family, and here in this walled prison the notion was even more alarming. He felt terror creeping over him. Where was he going? Would he ever see his parents again?

"John!" his mother cried, holding him. "We will come and find you. We'll be with you as soon as we can." He clung to her neck, unable to respond. He had barely a moment to say goodbye to his parents before he was ordered into the line of boys and marched away.

Desperately, he searched the crowd of boys for familiar faces, and there suddenly was Beda. Though they couldn't talk, their eyes met, a brief but reassuring glance. At least John had his good friend nearby. As he lugged his suitcase down the road with the other boys, he thought about Budejovice, and he remembered the times when he had tested his courage by jumping from the streetcar, or by climbing the Black Tower.

Survival here, in this prison, would take a very different kind of courage.

A street in the town of Terezin today.

Chapter 25
In the Barracks

John eventually found himself in Barracks L417, the house for boys under the age of sixteen. Because he was older, Karel went with their father.

The first time John entered the dormitory, he was terrified. He already missed his parents and his brother. There were forty boys in the room, crammed into a very small space, but John felt alone.

As he stood there, uncertain and afraid, a young man walked up to him and reached out his hand. "Welcome," he said. "My name is Arna. I'm looking forward to working with you."

Almost immediately, John felt himself relax. Young Jewish men and women lived in the children's barracks as house leaders. Arna, a tall, good-looking young man, was the leader of this boys' room.

John had to adjust to a new reality of life in this harsh place. Three times a day he stood patiently in a long line, waiting to receive his tiny portion of food. In the morning, there was weak coffee. At noon, prisoners received some watery soup – on good days there was a potato in it, or a dumpling floating on top. For supper, there was more soup and a small bun. Hunger pains clawed at John's stomach, until they became so familiar that he couldn't remember what feeling full was like.

In the barracks, the bunk beds were piled three high, to enable forty boys to sleep in the crowded room. It was dirty and difficult to keep the bugs and rodents away. Soap was a treasure, hoarded for the rare times the boys had the opportunity to wash in cold water. With no hot water for washing, lice bred in the boys' clothing, hiding in the seams, biting them and spreading disease. Prisoners became ill on a daily basis.

In another room in the boys' barracks, Beda was having his own problems. Shortly after arriving in Theresienstadt, he had contracted scarlet fever, a serious disease. It had begun with an infection in his throat and had led to a high fever and a rash across his body. Left untreated, scarlet fever could be fatal. Fortunately, Beda was treated in a small hospital and within a few weeks he recovered. But the disease left him weakened and frail.

Beda's sister lived in the girls' Barracks L410. Even though their buildings were close, Frances and Beda rarely had a chance to see each other. Frances spent her days working. Her first job was in a bakery, sorting through the mouldy bread that was put aside for the Jewish prisoners. She hated the work. The hours were long and the conditions were terrible. Back at home, this rotten bread would have been thrown out in seconds. But here in this prison, hunger drove Frances to steal pieces of the bread for herself and her family. You can eat anything when you are starving, she realised.

Frances' skill as a seamstress became useful in Theresienstadt. After several months, she was transferred to a sewing room in the basement of the girls' dormitory. There she mended and patched uniforms, and made toys for the children of the soldiers. She carefully stitched pieces of cloth together to make stuffed animals. Jewish children will never see these toys, she thought sadly, as she looked down at her handiwork.

At the end of a long workday, she climbed the stairs to the crowded room that she shared with nineteen other girls. Here she collapsed, exhausted, on her bunk bed, trying to ignore the fleas and bed bugs that bit her. I miss my home, she thought desperately. I'm tired and hungry, and I miss my family. Does anyone outside these walls care at all about what is happening to us?

A drawing of prisoners as they arrive at Theresienstadt, carrying their possessions.

Chapter 26
Bobrick

In spite of the harsh conditions, some events in Theresienstadt gave the prisoners hope. Through their own efforts, the prison became a place where music, art and poetry thrived. These activities helped everyone, especially the children, put up with the misery of their lives. When they created art and music, they dreamed of home, and remembered happier times.

Though school was not permitted in the camp, the adults were determined to continue educating the young people. Every day, the children learned from talented fellow prisoners – artists, writers, musicians and actors. Lessons were taught in the attics of the barracks, where the guards were less likely to discover them. Older children stood guard at the doors, on alert in case the guards came close by.

There were no textbooks. Instead, the teachers talked to their pupils and encouraged discussions about maths, history and literature. The children wrote stories and painted pictures. They sang songs, and talked about a future when they would all return to their homes and resume their lives. They participated in plays and musical events. They had chess tournaments and political discussions. There were even some sporting competitions. In every way, the prisoners tried to turn their unbearable living situation into something positive and good.

One day, Arna gathered the boys of John's room together for a meeting. Over the months he had become more than a leader; he acted as parent, teacher, counsellor and friend to the boys, doing his best to help them grow into young men. "As difficult as it is to be here, we have to learn to survive," he explained. "We have to find ways to be creative and keep our spirits high." He suggested that they might produce a newspaper for themselves and the others. Anyone would be able to contribute articles. The newspaper was to be called *Bobrick*, a Czech word for 'beaver.'

Once a month, the stories, poems and articles written by the children would be collected into a single edition of the newspaper that would be circulated in the barracks for everyone to read. Everything would be handwritten, since there was no typewriter. When the paper was finished, Arna would gather them all in the room so that it could be read aloud, while the older children stood watch at the door. Just like *Klepy*, this paper would be created and enjoyed in secret.

John could not believe what he was hearing. A newspaper here in Theresienstadt? He thought he had left writing behind when he left Budejovice. He listened carefully to what Arna was saying – that the boys needed to find ways to be creative, that writing was a way to use your mind, a way to feel connected to other people and to fight against rules and restrictions. This was the same appeal that Ruda Stadler had made for *Klepy*, to all the children of Budejovice.

His mind wandered back to the days when he had been part of *Klepy*. He had felt so productive and motivated then. As soon as the meeting was over, he set to work. He wanted to contribute something to this newspaper. With a dull pencil and a dirty piece of paper, he sat in his bunk and wrote a poem that he would contribute to *Bobrick*.

It has been five years
Since the devil marched into our peaceful land.
Death has moved from house to house.
War has brought terrible times.
Mothers and daughters light candles,
Remembering those beloved
They will never see again.

John never saw Ruda in Theresienstadt, but he knew that Ruda would be proud. We are doing just what he inspired us to do at home, thought John. *Klepy* had allowed them to show their resistance in Budejovice, by using their imaginations. *Bobrick* would do the same thing here in the squalor of Theresienstadt.

An unknown artist's rendition of the bunk beds in a barracks room in Theresienstadt.

Chapter 27
A Special Ceremony

June 13, 1943

On June 13, 1943, John woke up knowing that he was going to be part of a very special ceremony – his bar mitzvah, the day when Jewish boys mark their passage from boyhood into the adult practice of religious activities. Synagogue services and parties usually mark the day. But not for thirteen-year-old John. Here in Theresienstadt, there would be no ceremony in a real synagogue, and no lavish celebration.

In Theresienstadt, religious ceremonies like bar mitzvahs were held in secret. No one wanted to bring too much attention to Jewish customs. While religious services were not flatly forbidden, they were not entirely allowed either. They just happened, whenever and however possible. Small 'synagogues' were created in attic rooms throughout the prison. Rabbis from different towns and villages gathered their communities and held services when they could.

On the morning of his bar mitzvah, John dressed in the best clothes he could find. He borrowed a white shirt fraying at the collar. He tugged on his shirtsleeves. They were short, but they would have to do. His trousers hung loosely around his waist, and he tried to ignore the hunger pangs in his stomach. These days, hunger was a daily occurrence. Thinking about it only made it worse.

John reached into his pocket, feeling for the small gold pocket watch and the fountain pen, gifts from his father and mother for this special day. How had they ever managed to smuggle these things into the concentration camp, he wondered. He pulled out the watch and looked at the time. He had to finish getting ready. Quickly, he licked his hand and smoothed down his hair, then wiped a dirt smudge from his cheek. He took a deep breath and moved outside his barracks, climbing the narrow stairs to the attic of a nearby building, where the ceremony would take place. On the way, he mouthed the Hebrew words he was about to recite, over and over. In the absence of prayer books, he had learned all the prayers by memory, working in secret for months with Rabbi Ferda to make sure his pronunciation was perfect.

As John entered the small, dimly lit attic room, his mother moved forward to give him a warm hug. "We're so proud of you," she whispered, squeezing his arm.

His father nodded encouragement, while his brother punched his arm playfully. "You'll be fine," said Karel.

John glanced around the room. There were only about ten people there aside from his family – mostly friends from Budejovice. A couple of the boys from his barracks were also there, offering moral support.

John moved to the front of the small room to stand next to Rabbi Ferda, who smiled, his gold teeth catching the light from a candle that glowed on the table.

"Welcome, everyone," Rabbi Ferda began. "Today we are here to celebrate John's bar mitzvah. I have had the pleasure of knowing John since he was a small boy, and what a fine young man he has become."

John squirmed.

"Even though we are far from our home, our tradition is strong," the rabbi continued. "The prayer that John will recite today begins with a statement of faith in the future. And that's what we all must have."

Faith in the future, thought John. After fourteen months of imprisonment in Theresienstadt, it was almost impossible to imagine a future. Would he ever go home again, back to his own room, not one he had to share with forty people? Would he ever return to a real school, play in a real park or go to a cinema? Would he ever have a full meal, and even seconds, instead of having to stand in line for a cup of watery soup and a lump of stale bread? It was so long since he had enjoyed these simple pleasures.

As Rabbi Ferda finished speaking, John took a deep breath, closed his eyes, and began to recite the Hebrew blessings. He sang his portion perfectly.

Months of practice had paid off. His parents beamed with pleasure. Later, his mother sent a postcard to her sister in Austria, telling her that they were still well, and bragging about the wonderful ceremony for John. It would be the last message she would be able to send.

An artist's sketch of a religious service in the attic of one of the barracks. John had his bar mitzvah in a room like this one.

Chapter 28
A Wedding in Theresienstadt

In another part of Theresienstadt, Ruda and Irena were struggling to survive. Too old to be in the boys' barracks, Ruda had an exhausting job working in the bakery, with long hours and terrible conditions. This

A sketch of Ruda working in the bakery in Theresienstadt.

Frances lived in the girls' dormitory in Theresienstadt.
This is how it looks today.

isn't a bakery at all, he thought, remembering the
wonderful smells of the bakery at home. He tried to
keep memories of home as far away from his mind as
possible. But every now and then, he paused and
recalled the days when he and the others had worked
on *Klepy*. He had not written anything since he had
stepped down as *Klepy*'s editor. It was as if that part of
his life was finished.

Irena had been assigned to work with the young
girls, many of whom were orphans. Their innocent
faces longed for comfort, and Irena loved them and
looked after them as if they were her own children. She
called the girls *tetky*, a Czech word for 'little aunts', and
they lovingly and jokingly called her *strejdo*, which

means 'little uncle'. But despite their smooth young faces these girls were frightened, and Irena could do little to reassure them.

Each day, Irena received a small amount of bread to share with the children she cared for. "You cut the bread, *strejdo!*" the girls would shout. "Only you can cut the slices thin enough. That way, we can pretend there is more for all of us."

Irena would cut the bread into paper-thin slices and hand them to the starving children. "Here, my *tetky*," she would say. "Let's pretend this is a feast." She would smile, but inside she would wonder and worry about how long they could stay alive in there.

Ruda bent over the hot bakery ovens, hoping he would see Irena later that day. He visited her as often as he could. It was always difficult with family visits restricted to several hours once a week, but that did not stop him. He was clever and resourceful. He sneaked out late at night, travelling through the dark streets to Irena's barracks, dodging the guards on patrol with their fierce dogs.

"How are you managing?" she asked when he met her that night. She worried so much about her brother, who looked pale and thin.

Ruda shrugged his shoulders. "I'm still strong," he replied. "And you must stay strong as well." He reached into his pocket and pulled out a small loaf of bread that he had managed to sneak out of the bakery. "Here," he said. "I'll bring you more whenever I can."

He paused. "Have you heard the rumours? People say the transports leaving from here are taking prisoners to other concentration camps, where they are being killed." Each day, thousands of prisoners received notice that they were to be sent to an unknown destination in the east. No one wanted to talk about where that might be.

Irena nodded. Of course she knew about the transports to the east. But like most of the prisoners in Theresienstadt, she tried not to think about them. Besides, these days she did not want to talk about transports or death camps. In spite of the hunger, the misery, and the uncertainty in which they lived, Irena had fallen in love. Viktor Kende was a young man she

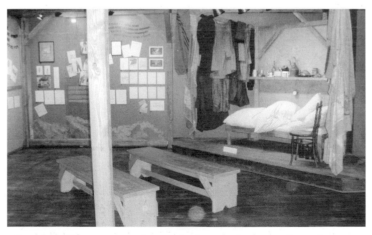

People in Theresienstadt watched ceremonies performed in attic rooms like this one.

had met in Budejovice. In the midst of the bleakness of Theresienstadt, their love had flourished. Finally they had managed to marry.

Viktor and Irena had wanted desperately to create a celebration for their wedding day. For days, they had hoarded extra food for the occasion. They had even managed to find some wine to add to the festivities. Irena had borrowed a white dress from another young woman in her barracks. Viktor had borrowed a suit that fitted his tall, handsome body almost perfectly.

On the day of their wedding, Ruda was there to rejoice with his sister, along with his parents and a few friends and family members. Once again, their beloved Rabbi Ferda conducted the ceremony in the attic.

A painting of Viktor and Irena
on the cover of their wedding book.

As the rabbi recited a blessing for the bride and groom, Irena closed her eyes and dreamed of their synagogue back home in Budejovice, with its lofty archways and beautiful stained-glass windows. Then she opened her eyes and looked up at Viktor. She reached for her new husband's hand and held it tightly. The Nazis could not stop this couple from loving each other. She and Viktor drank wine from a small glass, and kissed each other under a wedding canopy made from blankets and old pieces of clothing.

After that, Ruda wrapped a glass in a small piece of cloth and placed it under Viktor's foot. The breaking of a glass was an important Jewish wedding tradition, reminding everyone, even in joyous moments, that life was fragile. In Theresienstadt, with its constant reminders of the frailty of life, this tradition seemed even more poignant.

As Viktor's foot stomped on the glass and shattered it, the guests shouted, "*Mazel tov!* Good fortune! May your lives be full of joy!"

Chapter 29
Leaving Theresienstadt

November 1943

As thousands of new prisoners arrived in Theresienstadt each day, thousands also left, having received notice that they were being transported east. The death camps were no longer just a rumour. Each transport took several boys from John's room, and as each boy packed his meagre belongings and said goodbye, the others were left to wonder anxiously when their turn would come. Elsewhere in the world the tide of war was turning. Hitler's armies were losing in Russia and Italy. Surely they would be beaten, but would it be in time?

For the longest time, John and his family, and Beda and his family, as well as Ruda, Irena, and others managed to avoid the yellow deportation slips that would send them to the east. Because John's father was a doctor, his services were still needed in Theresienstadt. Beda and Frances' father had suffered a leg injury while doing forced labour in Budejovice, and that enabled him to delay his family's transport. Viktor Kende was able to keep the Stadler family safe. He had a job in the Theresienstadt transport department, which let him prevent some family members from joining the trains.

But they could not all avoid the yellow slips forever. On one cold day in November 1943, John and his family, along with thousands of others, received orders that they would have to leave Theresienstadt.

John stared at the little slip of paper and began to shake. The boys in his room were quiet, looking sadly in his direction and silently giving thanks that they had not been the ones selected.

John's mother came to help him pack for the journey. She pretended to be cheerful. "Another train ride," she said, smiling faintly. "But it won't be for long. We'll be home soon. You'll see."

This time, John was not fooled. He was scared.

The next day, he said goodbye to the boys in his barracks.

At four o'clock a.m. he and the others boarded their trains. These trains did not have seats. They were cattle cars – dark, cold and filthy. Families were pushed in until they were jammed together: men, women, and children. Finally, the heavy metal doors slid shut with a bang that echoed in the early morning air. The train left the station.

Their destination was Auschwitz.

Chapter 30
Life and Death in Auschwitz

John arrived in Auschwitz in November 1943. The next eighteen months of imprisonment was the worst period in his life. Auschwitz was a place of unspeakable horrors. There were brutal living conditions, constant disease, and daily deaths. John lived in what was called the family camp. Here, at least four thousand prisoners were crammed together in wooden barracks, with only boards as beds, surrounded by a fence of electrified barbed wire. The prisoners were starving. As meagre as the food had been in Theresienstadt, here in Auschwitz there was even less: one watery bowl of soup a day, with a small piece of bread.

The foul, muddy camp was a breeding-ground for fleas and other bugs. One winter day, John felt his whole body begin to itch and burn. He removed his jumper and looked at it closely. To his dismay, there were hundreds of tiny fleas crawling everywhere. It was as if the entire jumper was in motion, as the bugs danced across the strands of wool. This was his only jumper. There was only one thing to do. He shook the jumper wildly, and squashed the bugs between his fingers until he had killed as many of them as he could. Then, closing his eyes, he put the jumper back on.

Could anything be worse than this, he wondered. As each stage of his life became more unbearable than the one before, he would look back and long for past days. Compared to Auschwitz, Theresienstadt had been tolerable. Sleeping on a bug-infested mattress there had been better than sleeping on wooden boards here. Showering once a week, even in cold water with just a sliver of soap, had been better than no showers at all. The warmth of the boys' barracks had been better than this constant cold and never-ending mud. It was remarkable how one horrifying place could make another one look good.

Home seemed like a distant memory. He could barely recall the days at the swimming hole, and the happiness he had felt there with his friends. He thought about *Klepy* and the young people who had taken part in its creation, and he knew he had to continue to have hope. Hope was what had inspired the children of Budejovice to create *Klepy*. Hope was what had sustained them in Theresienstadt. But hope was harder and harder to find.

One day, shortly after arriving in Auschwitz, John walked outside his building. The frigid winter air passed easily through his flimsy jumper. He slipped and slid across the ice and snow in his thin-soled shoes, which had holes eaten through the bottom. It almost hurt to breathe, the air was so icy. But still, it felt good to be outside. He proceeded across the field, onto a small road in front of the barracks. The Nazis permitted these short walks, and this was the only form of exercise for his now weakened body.

As he walked down the road, he suddenly saw someone he knew walking toward him – a friend who had left Theresienstadt before he had. It was wonderful to see his friend, and to know that he was still alive, though frail and sickly-looking.

"Tell me what you can about this place," begged John. He was hungry for information, desperate to be reassured that things would be okay.

His friend shook his head. "It is worse than you can imagine," he said and John's heart sank.

It was this friend who told John about the gas chambers in Auschwitz. Thousands of Jews were herded into a large warehouse at one time, and the doors were locked. Deadly gas was then released into the warehouse. Each day, those who were sick or old or no longer needed were selected to leave their barracks for the warehouse. They never returned.

In July 1944, John's mother was sent to the gas chambers. Even as he hugged her and said goodbye to her, she did not cry. She shared a small piece of bread with him and held him close.

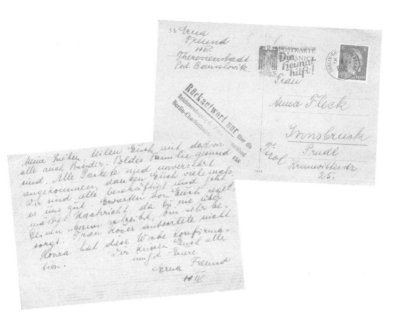

From Theresienstadt, John's mother sent this postcard to her sister in Austria. She writes that they are all well, and she talks about John's bar mitzvah. A few months later, the Freund family was transported to Auschwitz.

That same month, John said goodbye to his father and brother, and watched them being marched out of Auschwitz on a work assignment. They each carried a small loaf of bread and a few belongings. John waved at them through the barbed-wire fence.

It was the last time he ever saw them. He later learned that Karel had fallen from exhaustion while marching on the road, and had been shot to death on the spot. His father had refused to leave Karel's side and had been shot next to him.

Now John was all alone. He still fought to live,

with a strength he had not known he had. He went to bed each night and prayed to live to see the next day. Each morning, when he awoke, he marvelled that he was still alive. But how long could he hold on?

"Did you hear the news?" someone asked. "The Allies have invaded Normandy, in France. They are moving across Europe and pushing the Nazis back."

"I just heard a wonderful report," someone else said. "The Nazis have been beaten in Russia, and they are starting to retreat."

These scraps of information, whispered from prisoner to prisoner, provided renewed hope for John and the others. Maybe someday the Nazis would be defeated. Maybe someday this nightmare would be over.

Chapter 31

The March

April 1945

Day after day, news continued to trickle in that the Nazis were being driven back. The war had turned against Hitler. The Nazis knew they were about to lose the war, and they needed to hide the evidence of their crimes. John watched one day in amazement as the gas chambers of Auschwitz were torn down and destroyed.

And then new rumours started to circulate. The Nazis were moving their prisoners to camps deeper within Poland and Germany, trying desperately to evade the Allies, who were pressing closer.

In January 1945, all the able-bodied prisoners of Auschwitz were assembled in the open fields, and told that they would be leaving the camp. Along with thousands of other inmates, John was marched out of the concentration camp, and forced to march to a railway station fifty kilometres away. There they boarded open coal-trains that carried them to other concentration camps.

John spent two months in a camp called Flossenburg. From there, he and the other prisoners were ordered to set out again, marching to an unknown destination in the bitter cold, with little to eat, drink or keep them warm. They slept in open fields and barns, huddled together for warmth. The ordeal took one hundred days, but John was hardly aware of the passage of time. The hours, days and weeks went by in a blur. He walked automatically, placing one bleeding foot in front of the other, forcing a mechanical rhythm from his body that would keep him going. At night he closed his eyes, numb with pain, and then dragged his battered body into the cold for another day.

Many people fell ill around him. Hundreds of prisoners died each day, and their bodies were abandoned by the side of the road. John did not know how much longer he could survive. He had not eaten in days, and he had little strength. His time was running out.

One day in April 1945, just when he thought that he too might die, John looked up and saw American tanks approaching. Was this a dream? He rubbed his eyes in disbelief. With his last ounce of energy, he ran toward one of the tanks. A friendly American soldier lifted him up and handed him a chocolate bar.

The war was over.

John was alive and safe.

As soon as he was strong enough, John returned to Budejovice. He was now fifteen years old, and he was all alone. For three years he stayed in Budejovice, regaining his health. He returned to school, went to the cinema and attended concerts – all the things that had been denied to him during those long years of persecution and war.

He was also reunited with Zdenek Svec, the Christian boy who had steadfastly remained his friend. As she had promised, Zdenek's mother had kept the Freund family's belongings – his mother's fur coat, paintings, and rugs – safe during their absence. "Take them," she urged. "They belong to you." But to John, these things had little meaning. What good were fur coats and art? What he really wanted was his family. In the end, Zdenek's mother gave him some money for the

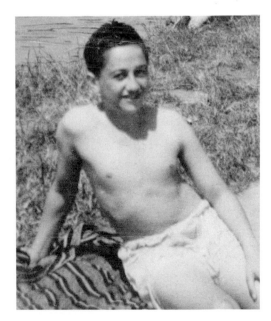

John was fifteen years old when the war ended and he returned to Budejovice. This photo was taken three months after his liberation.

valuables, so he could begin to make plans for his future. In March 1948, John left Czechoslovakia, and went to a country with a strange sounding name – Canada.

Before leaving Budejovice, though, he returned for a visit to the swimming hole. He stood on that familiar piece of land, and he closed his eyes and thought of those who were gone forever. First, he thought of his friend Beda. He could almost see him with his nose buried in a book, or contemplating his next chess move. Then he remembered Tulina, with her beautiful curls and her bright, warm smile. He thought of Rabbi Ferda, who had tried so hard to provide spiritual leadership for his community of families. And he thought of Joseph Frisch, who had been a good and dedicated teacher.

It was quiet by the river, but in his mind John could hear the sounds of his friends laughing, singing, playing sports and talking about the newspaper *Klepy*. He could almost see Ruda Stadler seated at his typewriter in the shed, surrounded by mounds of paper, or pacing with the other editors, discussing what to include in the next issue.

The Jewish children of Budejovice had been young and healthy, with strong spirits and boundless energy. They had had a deep love for their homeland, and a strong faith in their future. They had dreamed of growing up to be doctors, writers, musicians, or teachers. It had been unthinkable to them that they might die young instead. And yet not one of them was here today.

John remembered the blood contract he had signed with his friends, promising each other that they would meet one day in the future. That reunion would never be possible. He was the only one who had returned. He stood in the centre of their former playground and spoke their names aloud in a prayer to their memory. Then he turned his back and left the swimming hole for the last time.

A photo of John at the age of eighteen, taken on board the boat en route to Canada.

Epilogue
Finding Klepy

By the time the war ended in 1945, more than six million Jewish people had died, many of them murdered at the hands of Adolf Hitler and his evil Nazi colleagues. Of that number, it is estimated that as many as 1.5 million were children. Most of the young people who had been underground reporters in Budejovice did not survive.

Beda Neubauer went to Auschwitz, along with his parents, sister, and brother. Following the death of his parents and brother, Beda himself died in March 1944, his frail body fatally weakened by disease.

Shortly after arriving in Theresienstadt, Rita Holzer, the girl known as Tulina, was sent to the ghetto in Warsaw with her family. She died there.

Joseph Frisch, the teacher who had maintained a school for the Jewish children in his home, died in Auschwitz, along with Rabbi Ferda and most of the other Jewish families of Budejovice.

In September 1944, Ruda Stadler received his yellow deportation slip in Theresienstadt. He left Irena and Viktor behind and boarded the train for Auschwitz. From there he was transferred to another

This wood carving of a strong and heroic Ruda sitting on a loaf of bread (he worked in the bakery) was made in Theresienstadt.

concentration camp, where he was sent on a work detail. It was a bitterly cold day, and one of the guards at the worksite demanded the warm coat that Ruda was wearing. Ruda refused to give up his jacket. He was shot on the spot, having fought for his rights and his dignity until his last breath.

Irena and Viktor remained in Theresienstadt and were liberated from there at the end of the war. They were sick with typhus, a deadly disease transmitted by the lice that were rampant in the concentration camps, but they were alive.

There were others besides John who survived the war and began a new life. In July 1944, Frances Neubauer was sent to a work camp in Hamburg, where she sorted and cleaned bricks from bombed buildings, dug trenches, and built bunkers. In March 1945 she was sent from Hamburg to another concentration camp called Bergen Belsen. It was expected that she and everyone else would die there. Instead, Frances survived, and was freed on April 15, 1945. She spent the next few months in a hospital, recovering from typhus, but with proper medical attention she slowly recovered. Years later, she married a man named Lou Nassau. They moved to Australia and had two children and three grandchildren. In 1959 she and her family moved to Palm Springs, California, where she still lives today.

Frances Neubauer today, standing in front of the train station across from the house in which she lived before the war.

As for John, he arrived in Toronto, Canada in 1948, and over the next years he struggled to make a life for himself in this new country. He learned English, went to school, became an accountant, married, and had three children and ten grandchildren.

Sometimes, his mind would drift back to that other place – the country where he was born, the place that held those childhood memories of the swimming hole and the creation of *Klepy* – the place where the Nazis had taken away his freedom, imprisoned him, and killed so many of his friends and family members. It was strange to think of a place as happy and sad at the same time, but that was his memory of Budejovice – a place both joyful and tragic.

Periodically, John searched for survivors from Budejovice. He discovered that Frances Neubauer was alive, and began to correspond with her, recalling his days with Beda at the swimming hole, and the outings he had made together with other friends.

In the 1970s, John came across information that Irena Stadler was living in Prague. He wondered if she knew anything about the fate of the twenty-two issues of *Klepy*. Perhaps she knew whether Ruda had hidden them somewhere during the war.

He found Irena's address and tried to get a message to her. Since the war, though, Czechoslovakia had been dominated by an oppressive communist regime, with new rules and regulations. Communism was a political movement meant to give citizens equal opportunity for work, education, social class, and economic standing. In reality, communism was harsh and intimidating. Any citizen in possession of suspicious documents could get in trouble. John did not want to jeopardise Irena's safety, so he didn't ask her about the newspapers.

In 1989, the communist regime was overthrown, and John was finally able to visit his old homeland. He made his way to Irena's building, and climbed the stairs to her apartment. After ringing the doorbell with a trembling hand, he wiped the sweat from his forehead. He was sixty now, and the climb up the stairs had taken his breath away; his heart was pounding. In fact, this whole trip was physically and emotionally draining. He had not set foot in this country since March 1948. He had changed so much. Everything had changed so much.

The door opened, and there she was – Irena Stadler, now sixty-six years old, a tall, graying woman, still strong and clear-eyed.

After they greeted each other, he could not hold back his question: "Do you really have them?"

"I do," Irena assured him, her voice raspy, but firm.

"Can I see them? Please?" he asked, barely able to contain his impatience.

She nodded and moved down the narrow hallway. At the end of the hallway, she paused in front of a large cupboard. She opened the door, bent over, reached deep into the back of the cupboard, and pulled and tugged until she finally dragged out a worn brown suitcase. She carried the suitcase into the small living room, laid it on the floor, unlocked the latches of the suitcase with a loud click, and pulled the lid open.

John stepped forward to look inside. There it was.

Slowly he reached into the suitcase, pulled out the first bundle of papers, and read the title on the front cover – "*Klepy #1.*" Beneath this first set of papers lay twenty-one other bundles, neatly bound and perfectly preserved. The newspapers had survived.

John hugged Irena, and together they danced a crazy little dance around her living room, clutching each other. Thereza, the housekeeper with whom Ruda

A photo of Ruda's sister, Irena Stadler, taken many years after the war ended.

had left the newspapers, had kept them safe. Irena had managed to retrieve them after the war, and she had hidden them in her cupboard until this moment.

Now they sat down on the living-room floor and began to leaf through the pages of *Klepy*. John felt the weight of the stories in his hands, along with the lives of their creators. There were Ruda's editorials, the sports columns, the poems, and the beautiful drawings by Karli Hirsch. There was a photograph of John standing with one foot kicking a football. There were the stories written by his good friend, Beda, and the jokes about Rabbi Ferda and Joseph Frisch. There were pictures of Tulina, John's first love, and his brother, Karel, and all his other friends. It was a miracle that the

John and his childhood friend, Zdenek Svec, the one Christian boy who played with John against the orders of the Nazis.

John standing in front of the school in Budejovice that he
attended up until the third year.

newspapers had survived.

John stayed for many hours in Irena's tiny apartment, and returned several times after that. Before leaving Prague, he photocopied the entire collection of *Klepy*, and took the photocopies home to Toronto.

Some years later, John contacted Irena's son, Jirka, and discussed with him the best way to save *Klepy* for the future. They wanted other children to be able to see the newspaper and learn from its history. Eventually, Irena's children, Jirka and Hana, decided to give the entire collection of *Klepy* to the Jewish Museum in Prague, the Czech Republic.

It remains on display there to this day, for the whole world to see.

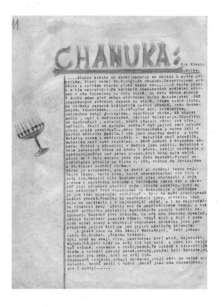

In this edition of Klepy, *an article about Chanukah includes the following passage: "Be proud of your people, so small yet so big, beautiful, and praiseworthy. Chanukah urges us to do good, noble deeds, and have strong character. The Chanukah candles shine back to the great past. Let them shine forth, so that while bringing back a memory, they also bring forth hope."*

Acknowledgements

Several years ago, I sat in John Freund's apartment and listened to him talk about a newspaper that he and other young people had written during the Holocaust. He showed me copies of the paper and he asked me if I would do something with his story. And so our journey began. It has been a privilege to work with John on this book. He is a caring and gentle man, who has patiently

John and the author (Kathy Kacer) standing in the central square of Budejovice.

and generously shared his life with me. Thanks also to his wonderful wife, Nora, for her strength and enthusiasm.

My deepest thanks to Frances Neubauer, not only for the open and honest way in which she talked about her life and the lives of her family members, but also for her warm hospitality. I will cherish the memory of my time spent with her in California. I am indebted to Jirka and Hana Kende for sharing their memories of their parents, Irena and Viktor, and their uncle, Ruda. They filled in the missing pieces of this story and helped ensure its accuracy.

The author, Kathy Kacer, and Frances Neubauer, standing in front of Frances' home in California.

I am grateful, as always, to Margie Wolfe of Second Story Press, for her enthusiasm and passion, and for her continued support of my writing. Thanks also to Laura McCurdy, Corina Eberle, and Peter Ross for their creativity and hard work in bringing this book together.

It is always a privilege to work with Sarah Swartz through the editorial process. Sarah is a wonderful adviser and a dedicated and diligent editor. Thanks also to Gena Gorrell for her final, thorough review of the manuscript.

I am grateful to the Jewish Museum in Prague, Czech Republic for providing photographs of *Klepy*, and to Patricia Tosnerova for her historical input.

Every time I feel overwhelmed with the writing,

John at the swimming hole today.

I am able to turn to my family for love and support. They remind me that this is all part of the process, and they calm and reassure me in ways that only family can. My love and appreciation go to my husband, Ian Epstein, and my children, Gabi and Jake.

Also available from the Evans Publishing Group:

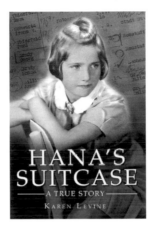

"I have been deeply moved ... highly recommended."
RABBI LIONEL BLUE

"Levine's account ... stands as a particularly poignant reminder ... and offers a vital lesson in the need for tolerance and respect."
THE TIMES

Other reviewers have said:
"A fascinating story ... highly recommended"
"Hana's Suitcase should be required reading"
"A must-have book"
"A remarkable book"

For more information on this or any other Evans titles, please contact Evans on 020 7487 0920 or visit our website www.evansbooks.co.uk. To order, please call our distributor TPS on 01264 343 072 or send a fax to 0207 487 0921.